*

The Conditions
for Educational Equality

*

OTHER TITLES

in

the CED Series

on URBAN EDUCATION

FUNCTIONAL EDUCATION
FOR DISADVANTAGED YOUTH

Supplementary Paper Number 32

RESOURCES FOR URBAN SCHOOLS:
Better Use and Balance

Supplementary Paper Number 33

The
CONDITIONS
for
EDUCATIONAL
EQUALITY

Edited by Sterling M. McMurrin

James L. Jarrett
Jerome S. Bruner
Staten W. Webster
James S. Coleman
Larry L. Leslie and Ronald C. Bigelow
Clark S. Knowlton

Committee for Economic Development
Supplementary Paper Number 34

A CED SUPPLEMENTARY PAPER

This Supplementary Paper is issued by the Research and Policy Committee of the Committee for Economic Development in conformity with the CED Bylaws (Art. V, Sec. 6), which authorize the publication of a manuscript as a Supplementary Paper if:

a) It is recommended for publication by the Project Director of a subcommittee because in his opinion, it "constitutes an important contribution to the understanding of a problem on which research has been initiated by the Research and Policy Committee" and,

b) It is approved for publication by a majority of an Editorial Board on the ground that it presents "an analysis which is a significant contribution to the understanding of the problem in question."

This Supplementary Paper relates to the following Statements on National Policy issued by the CED Research and Policy Committee: *Raising Low Incomes Through Improved Education* (1965); *Innovation in Education: New Directions for the American School* (1969), and *Education for the Urban Disadvantaged: From Preschool to Employment* (1971).

The members of the Editorial Board authorizing publication of this Supplementary Paper are:

This paper has also been read by the Research Advisory Board, the members of which under CED Bylaws may submit memoranda of comment, reservation, or dissent.

While publication of this Supplementary Paper is authorized by CED's Bylaws, except as noted above its contents have not been approved, disapproved, or acted upon by the Committee for Economic Development, the Board of Trustees, the Research and Policy Committee, the Research Advisory Board, the Research Staff, or any member of any board or committee, or any officer of the Committee for Economic Development.

CED RESEARCH ADVISORY BOARD—1970

Foreword

In recent years a considerable effort has been made to come to terms with the task of establishing educational equality in the United States. But this effort, which has been faltering and uneven and still shows few signs of success, has encountered far more difficulties than most had expected. These difficulties are not simply the familiar problems associated with equitable finance, the mechanics of integration, or even the cultivation of the human dispositions and attitudes essential to just and decent treatment in the schools. I have in mind, for instance, issues concerned with the meaning of equality, which have theoretic subtleties that demand the most careful philosophic examination, and those relating to the sociopsychological foundations of learning that will not be fully resolved until our scientific research and experimentation in the arts of teaching have moved far beyond their present state.

We are accustomed to speak rather casually of the imperative of educational equality, usually meaning equality of opportunity but recognizing the hazards of the egalitarianism that treats every person as if he were a duplicate of every other. But it has become clear, as the papers of this volume show, that it is not a simple task to refine the meaning of the common concept of equality of opportunity. Moreover, the material issues attending the achievement of the equal treatment of individuals are so dependent upon our knowledge of human development and behavior that a continuing extension of that knowledge, as well as more skill and wisdom in interpreting its practical values, are urgent demands. The celebrated Coleman report exhibited the extent of inequality in American education and revealed grounds for that inequality which had been hidden from most of us. It did this by identifying the social and psychological conditions that attend scholastic success and failure through correlating environmental and other circumstances with the degree of a child's achievement. Obtained on a massive scale, the findings, while subject to controversial interpretation, have pointed up much of our problem.

Here it must be remembered that we can no longer judge the issue of equality in education simply by school inputs described in such terms as money, buildings, equipment, or even the preparation of teachers. The primary consideration must be outputs measured in terms of actual achievement in literacy and other skills, knowledge, or motivation. And even the conception of inputs must be enlarged to include such social and psychological factors as a child's home cultural environment and the economic status of the families of his classmates.

The question of equality of education becomes immensely complicated when it is considered in relation to all these factors and with a concentration especially on the issue of poverty and matters of social and racial discrimination, whether overt or subtle. But unless this more difficult approach is taken, involving the full spectrum of the conditions relating to a child's learning, we will fail to get at the root of the matter, both in our attempt to define and understand the problem of equality and in our effort to resolve it by concrete decision and action.

Among many other things, this requires a thorough examination of various programs regarded as reformative or compensatory, with particular attention devoted to the worth of early or preschool education. It is now commonly held that children can learn more, faster, and at an earlier age than was formerly realized. Jerome S. Bruner and others have closely examined the psychological and other factors affecting pre-school learning, as well as the all-important relevance of early learning to later levels and rates of achievement; here is an area of great promise and one deserving continued research and experimentation. Many questions are still unanswered: at what age should schooling begin, under what conditions, with what techniques of instruction, with what kind of curricula, at what rates?

Indeed, if anything has become obvious through recent educational studies, it is that there exists an almost insatiable need for both basic and applied research productive of ideas and prescriptions for action that can be effectively demonstrated and packaged for useful consumption by the school educator. It must be research and experimentation that bring to the problems of education the kind of philosophic analysis that is exhibited in James L. Jarrett's chapter on equality, as well as research grounded on social, psychological, anthropological, and other sciences as represented especially in the other chapters in this volume. A clear and viable conception of the aims and purposes of American education is yet to be established, to say nothing of decisions on the substantive elements of the curriculum, the techniques of learning and teaching, and the institutional organization and control that are necessary and sufficient conditions for achieving those aims.

The papers that comprise the chapters of this volume issued from the Committee for Economic Development study which produced the policy statement *Education of the Urban Disadvantaged: From Preschool to Employment.* They may be read together with two other volumes from the same source—*Functional Education for Disadvantaged Youth* and *Resources for Urban Schools: Better Use and Balance.*

Perhaps it should be mentioned that the paper on the schooling of Mexican-Americans by Clark S. Knowlton has no counterpart here for blacks simply because the factors relating to the education of blacks have received extensive treatment in the other papers, as indeed in research generally. Mexican-American educational problems have been severely neglected as a national interest. The educational problems peculiar to American Indians are not studied here because the project of which these papers are a product was concerned with urban problems.

Sterling M. McMurrin, *Project Director*
Dean, Graduate School
University of Utah

Contents

The Conditions
for Educational Equality

*

1. The Meanings of Equality

James L. Jarrett

When Thomas Paine said that "inequality of rights has been the cause of all the disturbances, insurrections, and civil wars, that ever happened," he doubtless exaggerated.[1] But we do know that a vast deal of the world's social reforms have been conducted in the glare of this ideal's strident light and that at particular times *equality* has had an especial appeal, a point Alexis de Tocqueville made when he said:

> Democratic nations are at all times fond of equality, but there are certain epochs at which the passion they entertain for it swells to the height of fury. This occurs at the moment when the old social system, long menaced, is overthrown after a severe internal struggle, and the barriers of rank are at length thrown down. At such times men pounce upon equality as their booty. . . .[2]

Opinion differs as to whether such a revolution is today occurring, but there can be no doubt that many people of our time entertain for equality a passion that has swollen "to the height of fury." Even though fury is notoriously uncongenial to rational inquiry, we may hope to be pardoned for trying to understand this exceptionally complex concept.

Not as much has been written about equality as about freedom, yet the idea is a very old one, having fascinated thinkers at least from the time of the ancient Greeks. Indeed, Plato and Aristotle laid the groundwork for much subsequent thinking about equality—as they did on so many subjects.

Plato, for instance, recognized the difference between relative and absolute equality, noticing that things we call "equal"— say two sticks or two drawn circles—are only approximately and never fully so. Yet we have a conception of the ideal; we know what it means for two things to be equal, without ever having had experience of real equals. (Plato thought, by the way, that this curious fact constituted evidence for human preexistence.) Furthermore, in the *Menexenus* he expressed the Athenian ideal of a legal equality rooted in a natural equality of birth that recognizes "no superiority except in the reputation of virtue and wisdom." He was keenly aware of how, according to a might-makes-right doctrine, legal equality can appear as a nefarious scheme of the weak and the inferior to strip power from the naturally strong and superior; Callicles expresses this thought in the *Gorgias*. And he has Prodicus, Socrates' teacher and a Sophist famous for the niceness of his verbal distinctions, observe in the *Protagoras* that in a discussion the hearers should divide their attention impartially but not equally among the necessarily unequal speakers.

Perhaps most famously of all, in the *Republic* he adopts the meritocratic principle that there should be no initial discrimination among children with respect to deservingness of education. Even girls and the children of the poor and of the stupid should be given a chance, for they sometimes surprise us, and no state can afford to waste its resources for leadership. To be sure, he went on to say, inequalities will soon manifest themselves, and only those will continue their education who prove capable of the higher thought. Later in the same dialog, Plato strikes out at a kind of undiscriminating democracy that infuriated him: the supposition that all desires and all pleasures are equally good and legitimate and its equivalent in the sphere of social polity, that leaders should be chosen by lot, there being no real difference among men in political expertness. Although in his last work, the *Laws*, he recognizes a place for drawing lots to appease the masses by thus distributing minor honors and offices, he goes on to make a fundamental distinction between "two equalities under one name."

> The one equality, that of number, weight, and measure, any society and any legislator can readily secure . . . but the true and best equality is hardly so patent to every vision. 'Tis the very award of Zeus . . . . For it assigns more to the greater and less to the lesser, adapting its gifts to the real character of either.

Indeed, he goes so far as to say that "equal treatment of the unequal ends in inequality when not qualified by due proportion" and stirs civil discord. That distinction between quantitative and qualitative equality, the latter marked by "due proportion," it will profit us to hold in mind.

Similarly, in the *Politics*, Aristotle recognized inequality as everywhere a "cause of revolution" but especially in those cases when men who are really no better than their fellows claim the right to rule them. He too thought of equality as properly bound up with the concept of justice, which admits of numerical inequality so long as a right principle is employed. For instance, some men deserve better flutes than others; it is just if the best flutists get the best instruments, unjust if the richest do.

But the cases of Plato and Aristotle make us realize how hard it is to be truly universal in one's theory of equality. Can people who speak a non-Greek language and are therefore (by definition) barbarians be thought to warrant inclusion in the claim for equal protection of the laws or just deserts? No doubt a state should be organized so as to promote happiness of the citizenry, as Aristotle said, but beasts and slaves being incapable of achieving rationality, man's *arete*, or peculiar excellence, are thereby shut off from true happiness.

However, the highest expressions of Hebraic and Christian ethics transcended this parochialism, embracing all men in their conception of duty, law, justice, and equality by invoking the principle of universal brotherhood as a corollary of one God being the father of all men. Although I understand that there is no word for equality in Biblical Hebrew, one finds in Leviticus such a passage as this: "Ye shall have one law for the stranger and citizen alike; for I the Lord am your God." And the New Testament contains the egalitarian statement that "there is neither Jew nor Greek, there is neither bond nor free, there is neither male nor female: for ye are all one in Christ Jesus."

In our own time, Isaiah Berlin said that in its simplest form the ideal of complete social equality embodies the wish that everything and everybody should be as similar as possible to everything and everybody else. But most theorists have denied this or have preferred a much more sophisticated egalitarianism, agreeing with John Dewey that the ideal of equality does not mean anything so silly as absolute identity in treatment of different beings; rather it requires that every human being warrants equal *consideration* of his needs and wants. The baby of a family is an equal member of the family, he says, not in requiring the same food and clothing, but in that his interests and welfare may not legitimately be subordinated to those of the more powerful members of the family.[3]

Superficial though they be, these glimpses into the past reveal something of the length and breadth of man's fascination with the richly ambiguous concept of equality, for all of G. K. Chesterton's saucy observation that the British workingman was much less interested in the equality of men than in the inequality of racehorses.

Characteristics, Abilities, and Equality

Yet even within the realm of human equality and inequality, we must begin with what may be described as the factual—that is, the measurable, the scientifically specifiable. Men differ, after all, in height and weight and the color of their skin, hair, and eyes; they divide—at least roughly—into two sexes. In differing they are unequal. They differ, too, in non-physical ways, such as in personality, temperament, character, disposition, interests, desires, ambitions, tastes. Now, some of these physical and nonphysical characteristics are genetically determined in part or wholly. Others are acquired through the process of enculturation and socialization that anthropologists and sociologists like to talk about, or, more generally, through learning, which all of us like to talk about. This very distinction itself invokes the other distinction between the realm of plain fact and the realm of value, for it is not doubted by anyone that the color of our eyes is determined by genes. It is a biological impossibility for a brown-eyed child to have had two purely blue-eyed parents; but my hazel-eyed daughter has suddenly acquired most amazingly green eyes through the help of her oculist, and this new fact betrays a value: she *wanted* green eyes. Our so-called natural endowments tend to be modifiable, and we achieve modification according to our own or others' values.

It is useful to distinguish between such characteristics as we have presently been examining and abilities, even though obviously the two shade into each other. Among abilities, too, there seems to be a useful distinction between the inherited and the acquired. Thus, I have normal hearing ability but subnormal sight, and these sensory acuities are, I think, the way they are pretty much because of what came down to me from parents and grandparents, and very little because of maternal injunctions about washing my ears and not reading in the dark. On the other hand, whatever modest ability I possess to listen critically to music—to distinguish, as the famous limerick has it, between God save the weasel and pop goes the queen—has certainly been acquired.

Equality and inequality relate not only to characteristics and abilities but quite obviously to our material possessions as well. In a somewhat parallel though not identical way, here likewise we may distinguish between what one has to start with and that which one acquires. So too with our social groupings or, more generally, our social acceptability. One may be an American either by birth or adoption, and so too with respect to political party, socioeconomic class, and other groups that help give us our identity and a sense of being better off or less well off than our fellows. He who can complain that he has been denied the courtesies, the respect, that all can claim as rights in a civilized society has a moving grievance indeed.

Another realm in which persons have historically bemoaned or justified inequality is that of freedom, here taken to include what is sometimes called positive freedom, or power. To be forbidden by law to speak up, to change jobs, to vote, to travel, to go to the school or college of one's choice, to live where one likes is to be made aware of hard inequality in a generally just society.

Yet again, to be shunted off into jobs that are lowly, uninteresting, or poorly paid is to wonder wherein one has merited such a fate.

These latter kinds of groupings are inextricably associated with values and with status, though this is not to say that opinions are unanimous in rating the values. A member of the intelligentsia may pride himself on this identification, yet by no means necessarily be envied by jet-setters or activists. The middle class has in recent decades come in for a great deal of spoofing, and even contempt, for all of being the longed-for destination of millions of the poor. Or, an Oxford graduate may discover that his painfully acquired accent alienates him from the working-class companions of his youth. Possessions are sometimes decried as an encumbrance to virtue; indeed, it has been remarked that today's New Left may be the only instance in recorded history of revolutionaries who are both affluent and hedonistic. Even freedom and power are not universally sought and have sometimes been voluntarily sacrificed or foresworn in the interest of security, contemplation, or even femininity.

This listing of respects in which people are equal and

unequal—physical and nonphysical attributes, abilities, possessions, social groupings, and freedom or power as well as
economic, political, and social privileges—might be either expanded or contracted. But what is immediately clear about any
such list is the fact that the categories are not discrete. Doubtless
there are some persons who are handsome, intelligent, rich,
prestigious, and powerful, and it might be possible to construct
a case showing that each of these qualities in some one individual had been independently achieved or inherited. But it is
far more usual for prestige to owe a good deal to wealth, power
to intelligence, and so on. At the other extreme there are not a
few in the world who might fairly be described as ugly, stupid,
poor, lowly, and helpless; again, these attributes assuredly tend
strongly to influence each other. The result of these interactions
and reinforcements is, of course, that inequalities tend to get
increased, since superiority in one respect begets superiority in
others; so too with inferiorities or deficiencies.

Now, as has been noted already, human differences may be
either neutral or invidious. Physical characteristics in some
contexts, for instance, do not call out either envy or pity, and
are not a basis for serious differential judgment. Every person
has unique fingerprints, but to compliment someone on his
pattern would have to be an in-house joke of the FBI. In a
relatively heterogeneous and mobile society, many persons
tolerate a fairly wide divergence of bodily sizes and shapes,
color of eyes and hair, and other physical attributes, and though
each may have his personal preferences, he can see these as
idiosyncratic and irrational. ("Do you really prefer the willowy
type? That's funny, for I don't at all." And so on.)

But everyone knows that catholicity of tolerance and taste
in one's fellow human beings is hard to come by and hard to
sustain. A pretty substantial history of civilization could be
written about the vast capacity of human beings (and of course
other animals, too) *not* to be neutral in their distinctions. As
long ago as the sixth century B.C., the Greek philosopher Xeno-

phanes noted the silliness of anthropomorphism in saying, "Aethiopians have gods with snub noses and black hair, Thracians have gods with grey eyes and red hair." In *Gulliver's Travels*, Jonathan Swift had no trouble in convincing us that factions could arise and go to war over whether the boiled egg should be cracked on the little end or the big end. And for all of our belief that a basic moral distinction must be drawn between that about persons which is accidental and that which is deliberate and essential, Aristotle noted that it is hard for an ugly man to be happy. Certainly in most societies it has been very hard to be happy if one differs more than the small allowable amount from the prevailing standards of physical appearance, as well as of religious belief, moral habits, and even interests and tastes.

Now, those who have urged reforms under the ideal of equality have typically sought both to reduce differences and to dismiss differences as unimportant. The paradox is of course entirely superficial. Differences between individuals and groups with respect to possessions are always theoretically eliminable, an ideal widely held by parents with respect to their children. Certain freedoms can be extended to whole populations, as by the American Bill of Rights. Certain social groupings can be outlawed (e.g., fraternities in high school) or debunked. But other differences, especially physical differences, may be neutralized. Thirty years ago in our society, tall women frequently slouched, but fashions changed: today even very tall women may wear their hair piled on top of their heads. A more interesting example is the new acceptance by blacks of the natural color of their hair and skin. Only a few years ago the birth of a child in many black families was an occasion of anxiety, with resulting gratification or disappointment depending on the relative lightness of the infant's skin. I would judge that this phenomenon has changed radically in a short space of time, and may well give egalitarians hope for removing many other invidious distinctions based upon such physical attributes.

The case of abilities is more complicated. I assume that in every society certain human abilities are particularly prized and that the unequal distribution of these abilities constitutes one basis for esteem and disesteem. In our own society I should think that evidence of unusual musical ability would normally be occasion for congratulation; but the lack of such ability is certainly no disgrace. Indeed, except in such contexts as compulsory choral singing, even gross deficiency in this respect is not thought to be a heavy burden to bear through life. So, too, with many other abilities. This is perhaps because it is generally thought that one can normally compensate for one *de*ficiency by another *pro*ficiency. ("Does your boy play the violin? Well, mine loves to build things.") The case of intelligence appears to be somewhat different, particularly because it is a very *general* attribute. Although here, too, most persons seem able to accept in themselves or their relatives some degree of shortcoming (siblings' IQ's after all correlate only about +.5) gross deficiency in intelligence is certainly thought disastrous by many people.

In this latter case, an important question can arise as to whether inequality of intelligence should appropriately call out the egalitarian response of toleration of differences ("Some people are tall, some short; some bright, some not; and that's the way it is.") or of *reducing* differences. If intelligence, like height, is largely a matter of inheritance, then presumably one's moral obligation is to learn to live with all the differences that in fact there are and not to make these differences the basis for limiting anyone's rights.

But for the last several decades there has been a very strong tendency to take another tack—or rather one of two tacks. In certain circles today, it is popular to deny the existence of any such general trait as intelligence, and to say instead that there is a considerable number of relatively independent traits that tend to get lumped together. This group would have us acquire the habit of always qualifying the word *intelligence* by a modifier, so as to speak of spatial intelligence, social intelligence, quantitative reasoning intelligence, verbal intelligence, and so on. If indeed, as is maintained in some circles, there is a sizable list of such abilities, with no very high positive correlation among them, this tends to leave open the possibility of compensating for a lack of ability in one respect by an above-average ability in another, and so seriously mitigate the stigma associated with the word *unintelligent*.

Another possibility is to say that intelligence is not, or not primarily, a genetically derived physical capacity, like height, but is a learned capability. Thus, with only rare exceptions (e.g., brain damage) every person on birth has the capacity to function within the so-called normal range of intelligence. This is a moderate environmentalist view. An extreme position is that any person is capable of being taught to become a "genius."

Understandably, those persons who are strongly motivated by the ideal of equality incline strongly toward one or the other of these two interpretations of intelligence, either denying any such general trait or asserting that intelligence is principally or wholly learned. (Or, of course, one may take both positions.) Both interpretations tend to debunk intelligence tests. In the first view, the intelligence test overemphasizes one or two of the abilities important to human functioning, such as abstract reasoning or verbal learning. In the second view, it turns out inevitably not to be a test of *native* capacity—there being ex hypothesi no such thing or at least no determining degree of such—but only an achievement test; it therefore discriminates against persons who have very different backgrounds from those of the dominant group, or against those who have had insufficient stimulation and development of their abilities.

The upsurge of environmentalists has been so striking in recent years that now those who put considerable emphasis upon the genetic basis of intelligence (regardless of what intelligence is thought to *be*) and who think that native endowment, in this as in many other respects, is modifiable only to a relatively small extent, find it difficult to get a fair hearing from their scientific colleagues and are often rejected out of hand as obviously bigoted by many egalitarians. It is only fair to add that inegalitarians are, in turn, strongly *disposed* to accept an account that emphasizes inheritance of mental abilities.

I have several times used the expression *egalitarian*, but I should now admit that this is a very loose term indeed. An egalitarian is by definition one who frequently appeals to some ideal of equality to support certain value judgments; but we have already explored enough of the ambiguity of this concept to realize that a great many different things can be—and in fact are—meant by equality. Furthermore, egalitarians are often interested only in certain kinds of equality or concerned with the injustice of unequal treatment of only certain groups or persons. History is full of persons who demand the removal of inequalities for all members of a certain class (women, students, Greeks, Aryans) but who remain relatively indifferent to the inequalities suffered by others. Or who are extremely vigilant about legal or political equality but oblivious of or even opposed to economic egalitarianism—or the other way around. It is not uninteresting, for example, that Lenin once said, "Any demand for equality which goes beyond the demand for the abolition of classes is a stupid and absurd prejudice."[4] In noticing this fact, however, I do not at all suggest that there is anything inconsistent about such selectivity within the wide range afforded by the ideal of equality; or that, conversely, having invoked the ideal for one kind of judgment, a person has any obligation to feel committed by it in very different contexts.

The Concept of Equality of Opportunity

A particular emphasis in modern times has been upon a kind of equality that we have so far only referred to glancingly, a kind often invoked—even passionately invoked—by persons who are strong in their insistence upon the inevitability or even the justice of inequalities of a different kind. I refer to *equality of opportunity*. Briefly, this ideal seems to mean that—whatever the case with respect to the unequal distribution of characteristics, abilities, possessions, the variation in social class or the range of power—no man should be denied the possibility of improving his lot. There ought to be a general condition of openness, such that anyone can by a conscientious effort better himself, and indeed that there should be no limits set to possible improvement—certainly no limits set or supported by law.

I cannot determine who invented this idea, but it may be said to be implicit in Jefferson's famous and wonderful change of Locke's statement of the basic human rights of life, liberty, and property to read life, liberty, and the *pursuit of happiness*. To have the right to determine the conditions of and to pursue one's own happiness seems to me to mean that the laws will not close one in. The opportunity to set and seek one's own ends and purposes will remain available to the high-born and the low, to the weak and the strong, the intelligent and the unintelligent, the rich and the poor, the well-favored and the ill-favored, without respect to race, color, or previous condition of servitude.

Furthermore, the importance of opportunity for betterment has long been closely associated with education. Aristotle called upon the state to assume responsibility for educating the whole free populace, at least in the rudiments of learning, primarily in the interests of improved citizenship. By the seventeenth century, Comenius could proclaim both the necessity and the possibility of educating everyone to know everything, a claim which outstripped all others until revived in our own time by the psychological behaviorists. Horace Mann was somewhat less sanguine about the educability of the populace, but he did trumpet forth the virtues of education in furthering progress toward economic justice, as in this passage:

> Surely nothing but universal education can counterwork
> this tendency to the domination of capital and the servility

of labor. If one class possesses all the wealth and the education, while the residue of society is ignorant and poor, it matters not by what name the relation between them be called; the latter, in fact and in truth, will be the servile dependents, and subjects of the former. But if education be equally diffused, it will draw property after it by the strongest of all attractions; for such a thing never did happen, and never can happen as that an intelligent and practical body of men should be permanently poor . . . .[5]

In short, universal education will open up opportunities to get ahead. No people has more strongly believed this proposition than Americans, a fact most eloquently testified to by the effort made especially from the time of Horace Mann.

All the same, it is common knowledge that it has been a heartbreakingly slow process to gain educational opportunity for those children who are intellectually gifted though poor, and it remains true even today that a significant proportion of our very best high school students do not go to college. It has been hard to break down the belief of earlier centuries that females are spoiled by any instruction that goes beyond the domestic arts and perhaps a little genteel watercolor painting or playing on the spinet. It has been hard indeed to raise the sights of many working-class parents so that they can see beyond the most confining kind of vocational training for their children. Any one of these histories warrants telling, but let us here confine our attention to recounting some of the stages in the uneven progress toward equalizing educational opportunity for American children of minority races.

We know, of course, that the great preponderance of black slaves were kept illiterate and ignorant of aught but what skills they needed to perform their servile tasks. Their being freed did not immediately or automatically change this situation; when, indeed, with emancipation the very possibility of schools arose for those who had been slaves, some states hastened to pass laws expressly forbidding any such eventuality. Even after adoption of the Fourteenth Amendment in 1868, there were scant opportunities for educating blacks in the South, where private education prevailed. But gradually and painfully as public education gained ground, the necessity of schools for blacks was increasingly faced. In the South these were, of course, separate schools (as they mainly continue to be today); and however much the achievement of any schools at all signalized a kind of victory for some egalitarians, it did not take long for the question to be asked and pressed whether the laws were equally protecting the rights of any group of people who were segregated from the white majority. The legitimation of the "separate but equal" doctrine in *Plessy v. Ferguson* in 1896, a case having to do in the first instance with separate seating in public conveyances, was even then disputed by Mr. Justice Harlan's lone and eloquent dissent:

> In respect of civil rights, common to all citizens, the Con-
> stitution of the United States does not, I think, permit any
> public authority to know the race of those entitled to be
> protected in the enjoyment of such rights . . . . In the view
> of the Constitution, in the eye of the law, there is in this
> country no superior, dominant, ruling class of citizens.
> There is no caste here. Our Constitution is color-blind, and
> neither knows nor tolerates classes among citizens. In
> respect of civil rights, all citizens are equal before the law.[6]

Fifty-six years later the Supreme Court unanimously en-
dorsed this opinion, this time addressing itself directly to the right of black children to be admitted to the wholly white public schools of Kansas, South Carolina, and Virginia. The opinion of Chief Justice Warren is among the best known of recent times, and though vastly controverted (for instance, denounced by the congressional delegations of all the southern states), still the Chief Justice was not impeached. This opinion, among much else, officially testified to the importance accorded education in our day. Here is a crucial passage in *Brown v. Board of Education* in 1954:

Today, education is perhaps the most important function of state and local governments. Compulsory school attendance laws and the great expenditures for education both demonstrate our recognition of the importance of education to our democratic society. It is required in the performance of our most basic public responsibilities, even service in the armed forces. It is the very foundation of good citizenship. Today it is a principal instrument in awakening the child to cultural values, in preparing him for later professional training, and in helping him to adjust normally to his environment. In these days, it is doubtful that any child may reasonably be expected to succeed in life if he is denied the opportunity of an education. Such an opportunity, where the state has undertaken to provide it, is a right which must be made available to all on equal terms.[7]

It is essential to recognize that this sociologically correct statement about the importance of education in our society in mid-twentieth century is not just incidental intelligence introduced into the court's opinion, but the very kingpin of the argument. As long as education could be conceived to be mainly an ornament or essential only for a handful of professionals, such a crude approximation to equality as that formula which found separateness compatible with equality might make do. But let education come to seem of such importance that any deprivation in that area betokened deprivation that was economic, cultural, and moral, and there was bound to be a closer scrutiny of the position. The court conducted such a scrutiny and ruled that to separate blacks "from others of similar age and qualifications solely because of their race generates a feeling of inferiority as to their status in the community that may affect their hearts and minds in a way unlikely ever to be undone." So it concluded:

That in the field of public education the doctrine of "separate but equal" has no place. Separate education facilities are inherently unequal. Therefore we hold that the plaintiffs and others similarly situated . . . are, by reason of the segregation complained of, deprived of equal protection of the laws guaranteed by the Fourteenth Amendment.[8]

We all know of the events that followed upon this opinion: the enforcement of desegregation in Little Rock and elsewhere and the continuing attempts to use the economic power of the U. S. Office of Education to nudge recalcitrant cities, North and South, to abandon both de jure and de facto segregated schools. (This maneuver is widely believed to have cost one U. S. Commissioner of Education his job when Mayor Daley in his own inimitable fashion nudged back.) Fifteen years after this court case, we know that desegregation, not to say integration, has been enormously difficult to achieve, especially in those communities where large ethnic minorities are congregated— the more so where these minorities have swelled to majorities or near-majorities, as in Washington, St. Louis, and New Orleans.

But these difficulties aside, there was no resting place in the invalidation of the separate-but-equal position. For one thing it became increasingly important to egalitarians all over the country to reveal and attack more subtle discriminatory devices, such as required photographs on application forms, so that college admissions officers could make sure that "quotas" were not exceeded or that administrators would not, sight unseen, employ a nonwhite faculty member. As to queries from federal agencies regarding the number of minority students enrolled, college administrators began responding, with no little institutional self-satisfaction, that they kept no such records and could therefore not respond to such a question. But of course this kind of "color blindness," in Justice Harlan's phrase, fairly soon came to seem to many (though not to all) a kind of myopia, too, in that it made all the more difficult the compensatory programs that were just then beginning to become popular. For how could one conduct an effective campaign for admitting more black and chicano students and recruiting more faculty members from minority groups without abandoning the pretense that there was no way of telling who these persons were since they were really no different from the majority?

I think no one could deny that during the 1950's and 1960's this country has been engaged in a strong egalitarian movement respecting the place in our society of ethnic minorities and that that form of egalitarianism called equalization of educational opportunities has been especially prominent. Yet, equally, no one could reasonably pretend that this effort has been successful, at least as success is measured by the gratification or even appeasement of those who have felt most aggrieved by what they perceive as the gross inequalities and inequities of our system.

The Struggle for Racial Equality

At this point let us again broaden our inquiry beyond educational opportunity, since education is continuous with many other facets of society, and ask about both recent gains and remaining problems in this battle.

Anthony Downs says that by 1985 about one in seven Americans will be nonwhite, with "a sharp increase in poor non-white households headed by women in U.S. central cities. . . . " The unemployment rate among nonwhites is presently at least double that among whites in every age group. In 1970, it was estimated that 58 per cent of blacks under eighteen years of age live in a household with two parents and that some 39 per cent of blacks (compared to 18 per cent of whites) live apart from their mates. In 1970, the median nonwhite family income was about 64 per cent that of whites and only 28 per cent of blacks, in contrast to 51 per cent of whites, were classified as white-collar employees.[9] On the average the black doctor earns only about half as much as his white counterpart. Of the 3 million illiterates of the country a third are black.

Furthermore, the integration effort cannot so far be counted a success, although in the 1970–71 academic year 39 per cent of the black children in the South attended predominantly white schools, a sizable increase over a two-year period. Thomas F. Pettigrew says that "there is more racial segregation of schools today in the entire United States than there was in 1954 at the time of the Supreme Court decision."[10] It has been estimated that, at a minimum, two-thirds of all black students in the first grade nationally are in schools that are 90 to 100 per cent black, and four-fifths of the white children are in similarly predominantly white schools.*

Nevertheless, important gains can be shown. Between 1920 and 1967, nonwhite males gained in life expectancy at birth from only 45.5 years to 61.1 years, which though it is still considerably behind white life expectancy represents a better gain, absolutely, over that period, than for the other group. Between 1950 and 1970, the percentage of nonwhites attending college four or more years rose from 2.8 to 9.1, whereas the white gain was from 8.1 to 17.0.

The number of black families that between 1960 and 1970 entered the income bracket of $15,000 and over represents in percentage terms a spectacular increase, going from 0.6 per cent to 8.5 per cent, and the reduction of families in the most impoverished brackets is also gratifying, even though the poverty rate in 1970 for blacks was more than three times that for whites. Between 1960 and 1968 it has been estimated that there was a 27 per cent drop in substandard homes occupied by nonwhites. The median years of school completed by whites and blacks closed from 12.4 and 11.4 years respectively in 1960 to 12.7 and 12.3 years in 1969.[11] Similar gratifying gains, absolutely and relatively, could be demonstrated in voter registration, decrease of maternal deaths, and a number of other

---

*For further discussion of this point, see Thomas F. Pettigrew, "The Educational Park Concept," in *Resources for Urban Schools: Better Use and Balance*, the second volume in the CED Series on Urban Education.

respects. Everyone knows at first hand the considerable moves toward equality by desegregation of the armed forces, public parks, playgrounds, libraries, golf courses and professional athletic teams; the diminution of restrictive covenant clauses in real estate contracts; the considerable falling off of the practice of denying accommodation to blacks in hotels; and so on.

Although I cannot cite figures, it is common knowledge in college circles that not only are admissions officers frequently waiving regular standards in the case of black and chicano applicants, but that nobody has so many or such good opportunities for employment on faculties as the members of ethnic minorities today emerging from the graduate schools. Whereas ten years ago the reluctance of administrators and teachers to group children in terms of ability was widely proclaimed misguided traditionalism, soft egalitarianism, and in general a vast disservice to the superior student, today everywhere tracking and streaming is under attack, not only in America but also in England, of all places. The reason: ability grouping is de facto segregation. This cheerful list could easily be lengthened.

However, the sobering fact is that dissatisfaction among the ethnic minorities has grown in recent years. One poll showed that the proportion of blacks regarding themselves as alienated from our society rose in only two years, from 34 to 56 per cent, the poll being taken just *before* the Martin Luther King assassination. The news of black militancy, often manifesting itself in breakdown in communication represented by so-called non-negotiable demands or in violence, is too recent to require recounting here. For anyone who expected that efforts in recent years toward greater equality of opportunity would be rewarded by widespread expressions of gratitude, not to say a complacent satisfaction among blacks over progress made, today's state of vast uneasiness must be particularly disenchanting. Undoubtedly, many whites who have through the years identified themselves as egalitarians with respect to the racial makeup of our society and who have worked in behalf of such causes as integration, today feel a letdown over the seemingly meager fruits of their efforts.

Concerning the many programs for early intervention in the education of the culturally different, the 1967 Civil Rights Commission reported, "A principal objective of each was to raise the academic achievement of disadvantaged children. Judged by this standard the programs did not show evidence of much success."[12] Those communities that have adopted so-called open-enrollment policies—that is, allowing students to register in any schools of their choice, thought to be a way out of de facto segregation—have apparently found that by and large pupils go to school where they went before. Reporting on a number of studies of special programs, Arthur Jensen states that, although spectacular results have been obtained in the relatively rare cases where there have been drastic changes in the schooling of students from extremely depressed environments, "Children reared in rather average circumstances do not show an appreciable IQ gain as a result of being placed in a more culturally enriched environment."[13]

As to the educational results of genuine integration programs, very little is as yet known, though egalitarians can take some satisfaction in James S. Coleman's finding:

> If a white pupil from a home that is strongly and effectively supportive of education is put in a school where most pupils do not come from such homes, his achievement will be little different than if he were in a school composed of others like himself. But if a minority pupil from a home without much educational strength is put with school-mates with strong educational backgrounds, his achievement is likely to increase.[14]

But as yet there has been surprisingly and distressingly little scientific evaluation of results. For instance, Berkeley, a city of 120,000, operates an integrated school district where not only schools but classrooms reflect the same proportion of white-black-Oriental persons in the community as a whole.

Although a sizable number of baseline data have been collected, it is unlikely that thorough and systematic follow-up tests will be conducted to determine the effect of this integration, at least partly because many members of the black community are understandably suspicious that an "objective" evaluation will turn out to be another "put down."

Some New Directions

So what lies ahead? It may be useful once again to search into the heart of equality for yet new directions. Perhaps this search can be put into the form of some tentative predictions, conjectural extrapolations of certain features of the current scene.

1. *The national concern for more effectively educating the culturally different and disadvantaged will increase rather than diminish.*

This will be the continuation of the trend that superseded the prior trend of a decade ago, when there was great concern for giftedness, honors programs, advanced placement, and so forth. It is interesting to read now the famous Rockefeller Report of 1958 entitled *The Pursuit of Excellence*, which said:

> Any educational system is, among other things, a great sorting-out process . . . . There is overwhelming evidence of a determination on the part of the American people that the sorting-out process be carried out mercifully and generously, rather than ruthlessly, rigidly or mechanically. But it has sometimes seemed that rather than admit differences in talent—or at least taking responsibility for assessing it—we prefer to accept mediocrity.[15]

Although there is no reason to believe that there is any necessary conflict between education of the gifted and education of the culturally handicapped, the words just quoted—to which at the time many responded with cheers—now sound strange to our ears. Today we are much more likely to be anguished by the evidences that the "sorting out" has already taken place—in large measure before children ever get to kindergarten. Our concern is that those who have been sorted out can somehow again be sorted *in;* or, at the very least, that their younger brothers and sisters can be saved from the sorry fate of achieving ineducability.

There may well be some serious repercussions to present militancy by blacks and students, particularly by black students. But I would regard it as in the highest degree unlikely that the nation will turn back from its determination to raise the educational attainments of that sizable number of students, mainly black and chicano, who are currently profiting little if at all from our schools and who are doomed by that to an inferior status, especially in our state of advanced technology.

2. *The concept of equality of educational opportunity will come in for strong criticism and consequent de-emphasis or revision.*

To too many people, "opportunity" has about it the conservative ring of passivity, a point made by political scientist John H. Schaar when he says that equality of opportunity "asserts that each man should have equal rights and opportunities to develop his own talents and virtues and that there should be equal rewards for equal performances. The formula does not assume the empirical equality of men. It recognizes that inequalities among men on virtually every trait or characteristic are obvious and ineradicable." But, he goes on to say, what this idea *really* means is that there will be "equality of opportunity for all to develop those talents which are highly valued by a given people at a given time. When put in this way, it becomes clear that commitment to the formula implies prior acceptance of an already established social-moral order."[16]

Furthermore, the emphasis upon opportunity will seem to some egalitarians to give comfort to those who like to say, perhaps with a sigh in their voices, "Well, we gave them the opportunity (free schools, open enrollment, special tutors, and the rest) and they simply didn't take advantage of it, or only the really exceptional ones did." Blacks today often express resentment of the singling out of exceptional blacks for commendation. This is sometimes called with withering scorn the "theory of supernigger"—that is, the supposition that only such blacks as Booker T. Washington and Martin Luther King are truly superior.

On the other hand, this concept is quite capable of being refurbished in such a way as to furnish a criticism of merely passive "opportunity." For instance, the point surely could be made that a person may die of malnutrition in the midst of plenty if he is grossly ignorant of dietary needs and that, more generally, for an opportunity to be *genuine* certain conditions must prevail. For instance, the child who has been conditioned by his society to think of himself as inferior, as a nonlearner, tends to act in an inferior way and to *be* a nonlearner.* Such a pupil is not at all likely to "take advantage of educational opportunities." It can be further argued that vast attention needs to be paid to more effective motivation for youngsters who are immobilized, as many seem to be, by a combination of indifference toward the prevailing values of a school and a sense of helplessness with respect to the society at large. Here again, the familiar but poignant point can be put that one cannot speak of opportunities really being present unless something has been done to make these opportunities attractive.

3. *Following upon such a criticism and possible reinterpretation of the concept of equality of educational opportunity, there will be a reexamination of various kinds of compensatory programs.*

Suppose again a concrete and typical situation. A university decides that its admissions standards (whether college

---

*There are interesting recent studies, such as that of Robert Rosenthal and Lenore Jacobson, to show how teachers who have already made up their minds that this pupil is bright, this one stupid, act so as to help fulfill their own implicit prophecies.[17]

boards, high school grade-point average, or whatever) are effectively screening out minority-group applicants. Recognizing the legitimacy of recent criticisms of practically all psychological testing as culturally biased, and also realizing how seldom black and chicano students achieve up to their capacity in the schools, the university will admit such applicants on other bases; e.g., character references or indications by high school teachers of "high potentiality." In addition, financial aid often will be provided and perhaps remedial and tutorial to help the student in getting started.

Such familiar procedures are of course susceptible of criticism as violating the ideal of equality by a reverse prejudice. But they are defended today, and will continue to be, as the kind of compensation necessary in the case of those who have long suffered from grossly unequal treatment. In other words, a university cannot effectively provide equality of educational opportunity now without bringing students up to the point of being able to take advantage of that opportunity.

4. *Colleges and universities will become more aggressive in seeking out more blacks and chicanos.*

Typically, when a university changes its admissions standards and announces that henceforth minority group students will be welcome to apply, essentially nothing happens. For instance, the Berkeley campus of the University of California traditionally has had exceedingly few black students even though it is located in a community about 40 per cent black and has low fees. Concerned over admissions standards and—perhaps even more seriously—over a certain reputation for being formidably intellectual, the university finds ways of letting students in who have not met those standards and it also makes efforts to appear less chillingly lofty. More black students come, but not many more. Similarly, with recruiting faculty. For a very long time, Berkeley and many other universities have been proudly nondiscriminatory in respect to faculty hiring. No doubt the wish has been often expressed that more candidates well qualified in the customary ways would apply, so that there might be an opportunity to make good on the claim that "other things being equal, we would actually prefer minority-group applicants." Few appear. So, as in the case of admissions, the university finds it possible to be less severe in what it requires in the way of degrees or publications. Even so, not very much happens.*

What we will begin to see in the very near future is a considerable stepping up of the process of active recruitment of ethnic minorities for student bodies and faculties. Black and chicano recruiters will seek out and offer various inducements to members of these groups to come to the colleges and universities. There will be more long-range programs to identify such students earlier; there will be more use of special summer programs to plant the seeds of desire for a college education and to encourage minority-group students to go on to graduate school to prepare for teaching and other public service careers.

5. *As the ideal of educational opportunity is extended, there will be a turning away from equality of input toward equality of output.*

Much has been said of the size of effort that has been made to equalize opportunity. Such and such a number of dollars have been spent; so many early childhood programs

---

*By the fall of 1970, black undergraduate enrollment at Berkeley was up to 4.5 per cent, an impressive gain from the 2.3 per cent of two years earlier, but still behind Princeton, Harvard, and Yale. Then, consider the astonishing growth at the University of Vermont: 0.1 to 0.4 per cent.

However, another recent development is discouraging. The new financial hardships of most universities and colleges are causing a sharp drop in the aid that is essential to recruiting among minority groups. For instance, at Berkeley a program for preparing urban teachers that had in its first two years enjoyed splendid success in recruiting blacks and Mexican-Americans for paid applicants have increased in number and in quality, but school districts are laying off regular teachers, not hiring interns. The same thing is true about scholarships, fellowships, loan funds, and work-study programs, whether from federal, state, or private sources. The drying up of these funds could by next year wipe out most of the gains of the previous three or four years.

have been set in train; this and that curriculum reform has been instituted to make the educational experience more meaningful to ghetto children; and this amount of in-service teacher training has been offered in the interest of more effective instruction. Here and there on the horizon there have been flashes of light, but by and large the results of these greatly increased inputs have been meager and the prospects remain dim.

The shift from equality of *input* toward equality of *output* can be given either a minimal or maximal interpretation, neither one involving a levelling down. That is, some critics of the schools have long believed that the typical teacher is already too much inclined to minimize differences. (There is indeed some truth in the oft-repeated story of the teacher who said that at the beginning of the year she couldn't do a thing with her class, so wide was their range of performance, but that she usually succeeded by the end of the year in speeding up the slow and slowing down the speedy sufficiently to make a nice class of boys and girls.) Very different, however, is the decision to achieve, in a given class, uniform success with respect to certain minimum standards. A good example is learning to read. In our society, there is no reasonable place for the nonreader. It would perhaps be fair to say, about a given first-grade class, that all the pupils *must* learn to read by June. That is, everything necessary will be done to make sure of uniform success in this respect. This may mean sacrifices with respect to the rest of the curriculum, in order to afford the employment of various technological aids, the use of special tutors, home visits, cajolery, bribery—or whatever else it takes. But all the students *equally* must learn to read. It is to be noticed that this is not to say that all the students must be taught to read equally well.

Whether this is indeed a reasonable and realistic expectation, in the case of first-grade reading, I am not competent to say with assurance, though I suspect it is. I give it as an example, however, of what could be decided upon—perhaps preferably with full pupil participation—as goals for every member of a class.

I am suggesting, in short, that there is a subtle but possibly critical difference between (1) "We have determined to equalize educational opportunity, including the provision of strong compensatory aids for disadvantaged learners," and (2) "We have determined to do whatever is necessary to bring all the pupils up to certain specified standards of performance."

Such would be a minimal interpretation of equality of output. A maximal interpretation would have it that the time is not far off when we will have the power to remove learning deficiencies by biological and chemical manipulations of the environment; so we had better be adjusting our ideals to allow for this kind of power.

David Krech, the distinguished psychologist, has recently reported that in his own experimentation he has proved that the size, weight, and texture of a rat's brain can be significantly changed by an enriched environment; while the experimentation of other physiological psychologists has shown that injections have improved rats' capacity to learn and to remember by 40 per cent. Krech's own (and inimitable) summary is that "here we have a 'chemical memory pill' which not only improves memory and learning but can serve to make all mice equal whom God—or genetics—hath created unequal."[18]

It is of course not yet certain that the same results can be obtained with humans. But at this point in time it would take a brave or foolish man to deny it categorically, a point on which I confess to being persuaded by the evidence that such "natural" inequalities as hair texture, eye color, and the measurements of female bosoms may be drastically modified. So likewise with what we have regarded—here I speak for those of us who have *not* been persuaded by the extreme environmentalists that the human mind is infinitely malleable through conditioning—as the "natural" inequalities of people with respect to their neural equipment. These, too, may soon be readily modifiable by chemical modifications of the brain or of the genes directly, as to eliminate the lower end of the present learning curve. I do not, of course, argue that such prospects relieve anyone from present obligations to continue working on educational and other means of raising the achievements of those whom the schools are today failing on.

6. *There will be a growing awareness of the dangers implicit in high competitiveness in the classroom and a search for ways of motivating students by individual goals.*

In the late 1950's and early 1960's, critics of American schools lashed out at dead-level mediocrity, heterogeneous grouping, automatic promotion, universal graduation of the merely persistent, and other school practices and attitudes they found to be stifling of "excellence." The reaction took the form of a new and heavy emphasis upon honors programs, enriched curricula, ways of identifying superior and talented pupils, and so forth. But with the rediscovery of widespread poverty, the outbreak of urban rioting, and the increasing recognition of the extent of early school dropouts and of functional illiteracy among underprivileged groups, attention shifted to the iniquities of educational inequality. One consequence has been a certain de-emphasis upon competitiveness in the schools and a suspicion of tests and measurements that purportedly reveal "natural" inequalities.

It appears probable that this tendency will continue, with increasing attention being paid to sharing, cooperation, and the attainment of whole groups, in sharp contrast to publicizing rank in graduating class and other such hierarchical ordering, especially as determined by culturally biased tests.

It is said that Pueblo children will not give their teacher an answer until everyone in the group is prepared to answer; such a cultural difference focuses attention anew upon the place of competitiveness in our schools. We are acquiring a better realization of the fact that individuals and groups often have qualities that compensate for certain academic deficiencies. Indeed, such an expression as *culturally deprived* may mean only deprived respecting the dominant culture. As astute a psychoanalyst as Erik H. Erikson has suggested that "the middle-class culture, of which the slum children are deprived, deprives some of the white children of experiences which might prevent much neurotic maladjustment."[19]

It would be unfortunate in the extreme if the ideal of equality of educational opportunity should blind teachers and others to the right of every child to have his distinctive interests, abilities, prospects, and aspirations—and those he may share with an ethnic group—taken sensitively into account.

7. *As students increasingly reject the paternalism of the schools and press for more autonomy, teachers and administrators at every level will have to find ways of "involving" students— not in a token or pro forma way, but deeply in what, after all, is their education.*

One of the strongest appeals which has been made to the human imagination is that of a society, even of a whole world, in which the members are equally autonomous—not only in that every nation or every group is the equal of other nations and groups in this respect, but that, person by person, autonomy should prevail. I cannot here enter into what this means, or might mean, politically, economically, or in many other ways; instead, I will touch upon a few of its educational implications.

To me, the most important element in the endlessly interpreted emergence of student dissidence is the groping for personal autonomy. Students all over the world and of every color are saying in various degrees of stridency, if I understand them at all, that they can no longer tolerate being looked upon as the mere *recipients* of an education; that is, having the content of their education (to say nothing of the medium, which we are told is really the content or message) decided by others than themselves, no matter how old, experienced, and wise those decision makers may be.

Now this is, I believe, what the underprivileged minorities of America are saying, too, with profound variations. But if the white, middle-class, materially secure young person finds himself unwilling to accept the paternalism of our educational system, how much stronger must be the case of the black student, the Puerto Rican student, the Mexican-American student, the Indian student, when he complains that he cannot accept the education that is being handed him by persons with whom he does not identify and increasingly does not want to identify. "Self-determination" is the cry.

Most recently this cry has taken the form of a demand for separate programs, separate departments, separate colleges, and now separate universities, with Third World faculties, no outside interference with admissions policies, evaluation, curriculum, and all the rest. High school students are beginning to follow suit. The irony of this return to the separate-but-equal formula has been commented on, but many people regard such an outcome as a disastrous culmination to the long struggle for equality; this probably still represents a very small minority of opinion. Thus, Thomas F. Pettigrew claims that 85 per cent of black adults favor integration and that there has been no change in this percentage over the past several years.

But such is by no means the only meaning that can be assigned to the word *autonomy*. Teachers and administrators are today groping with ways of involving students; there is no ready-made answer, and teachers must be taught, must teach themselves, how better to proceed. The supposition that only *adults* have gained the right to such autonomy is surely back of a lot of today's troubles; it is predictable that similarly stodgy thinking will block progress toward genuine involvement of young pupils—including the very youngest—in their own education. Those who indulge in parodies about kindergartners voting on "what we will do today" are not only quoting those who fought the important reforms of John Dewey a generation and more ago, but are muddying the waters of today's inquiry.

The answers lie not in votes and in power plays but in jointly conducted investigation.

A great deal has been accomplished in the name of equality. The general reach of laws and mores has been extended to include groups long relegated to a distinctly inferior status. More and more it is agreed that it is *un*equal, not equal, treatment that requires justification and that universality of rule is the best proof against arbitrary acts of discrimination or plain prejudice.

Progress is uneven and uncertain, but one is entitled to think that we have not yet seen the last innovation in the interpretation of equality. Nobody knows what might be next. It is foolish to try to make equality into the only ideal. The fact that a parent or teacher may evenhandedly mistreat or deprive all of his charges is a reminder that equality must be supplemented by justice, freedom, and a dedication to human weal. But if the struggle for human betterment continues, equality will be the banner to which we will continue to rally, with ever new meanings accommodated to its fecund ambiguity.

2. Poverty and Childhood

Jerome S. Bruner

I should like to consider what we know about the education of the very young—about what may be formative influences during infancy and early childhood upon later intellectual competence and how these influences may be more compassionately deployed. Our focus will be upon the manner in which social and cultural background affects upbringing and thereby affects intellectual functioning. And within that wide compass, we shall limit ourselves further by concentrating principally upon the impact of poverty and dispossession.

There is little enough systematic knowledge about what happens to children during infancy and early childhood and even less about how these early years affect competence later on. Indeed, in the current debates, it is a moot point as to what is properly meant by intellectual competence, whether or in what degree competence comprises soul, mind, heart, or the general community. Nor can the topic be limited to education. For the charge has been made by royal commissions and advisors to presidents as well as by the anti-establishment New Left that educational and socializing practice, from infancy and even beyond the school years, reflects and reinforces the inequities of a class system by limiting access to knowledge for the poor while facilitating it for those better off. The charge is

34

even more serious: that our practice of education, both in and out of school, assures uneven distribution not only of knowledge but also of competence to profit from knowledge. It does so by limiting and starving the capabilities of the children of the poor by leading them into failure until finally they are convinced that it is not worth their while to think about school-like things. As Susan S. Stodolsky and Gerald Lesser grimly put it, "When intelligence data and early achievement data are combined we have a predictor's paradise, but an abysmal prognosis for most children who enter the school system from disadvantaged backgrounds."[1]

Why concentrate on the very young? The answer is, of course, in the form of a wager. For one thing, Benjamin S. Bloom's careful and well-known work strongly suggests that a very major proportion of the variance in adult intellectual achievement, measured by a wide variety of procedures, is already accounted for by the time the child reaches five, the age at which he usually starts his schooling.[2] For another, there are enough studies to indicate, as we shall see, that certain possibly critical emotional, linguistic, and cognitive patterns associated with social background are already present by the age of three. But principally, I am moved to concentrate on the very young by my own research and by studies made with K. Lyons and K. Kaye.[3] The staggering rate at which the preschool child acquires skills, expectancies, and notions about the world and about people; the degree to which culturally specialized attitudes shape the care of children during these years—these are impressive matters that lend concreteness to the official manifestos about the early years.

Our first task is to examine what is known about the effects of poverty on child development in our contemporary Western culture—whether this knowledge comes from attempted intervention, from naturalistic studies, or from the laboratory. I do not wish to make a special issue of poverty, of whether or not it represents a self-sustaining culture, as the late Oscar Lewis urged;[4] nor do I want to make the claim that poverty is the same in every culture. Yet there are common elements that are crucial wherever it is encountered and in whatever culture it is imbedded. We shall have more to say about this as we consider how poverty and its attendant sense of powerlessness may affect the patterns of growth in children.

Our second task is to look briefly at modern theories of development with a view to assessing whether they help us to understand the impact of culture generally on growth and the impact of poverty in particular.

Finally, and again too briefly, we must examine the implications of this examination for public policy and for the conduct of early education. As Robert D. Hess and Virginia C. Shipman have written, "The current growth of programs in early education and the large-scale involvement of the schools and federal government in them is not a transitory concern. It represents a fundamental shift in the relative roles and potential influence of the two major socializing institutions of the society—the family and the school."[5]

Most of the work that compares children from different socioeconomic backgrounds points to three interconnected influences associated with poverty. The first influence relates to the opportunity and encouragement the child is given in the management of goal seeking and of problem solving; it reflects differences in the degree to which one feels powerless or powerful and in the realistic expectation of reward for effort. What the child strives for, how he goes about the task of means-end analysis, his expectations of success and failure, his approach to the delay of gratification, his pacing of goal setting—these are not only crucial, but they also affect how he uses language, deploys attention, processes information, and so on. The second influence is linguistic: by exposure to many situations and through the application of many demands, children come to use language in different ways, particularly as an instrument of thought, of social control and interaction, of planning, and so forth. The third influence comes from the pattern of reciprocity experienced by the child, which will differ if the milieu is middle class or poor and dispossessed. What parents expect, what teachers demand, what peers anticipate—all of these operate to shape outlook and approach in the young. We must consider each of these in turn.

Goal Seeking and Problem Solving

A close reading of the evidence surely suggests that the major source of cognitive difference between the poor and those better off, between persons who feel powerless and those who feel less so, lies in the different way goals are defined and how means to their attainment are fashioned and brought into play.

Let us begin with a general proposition: one feels competent about oneself before feeling competent about others or about the world at large. James Moffett observes how language complexity increases when the child writes or speaks about events in which *he* participated in a goal-seeking process.[6] Consider these unlikely initial subordinate constructions from third-graders uttered in describing a task in which they have had a central, directive role:

> If I place a flame over the candle, the candle goes out.
> When you throw alum on the candle, the flame turns blue.

Or let us take two speech samples from lower-class black children, one describing a television episode in "The Man From U.N.C.L.E.," the other a fight in which he, the speaker, was engaged:

> This kid—Napoleon got shot and he had to go on a mission
>   and so this kid, he went with Solo.
> So they went.
> And this guy—they went through this window.
> And they caught him.

And they beat up them other people.

And they went and then he said that this old lady was his mother and then he—and at the end he say that he was the guy's friend.

And the fight:

When I was in the fourth grade—no it was in the third grade—this boy he stole my glove.

He took my glove and said that his father found it downtown on the ground.

(And you fight him?)

I told him that it was impossible for him to find downtown 'cause all those people was walking by and just his father was the only one that found it?

So he got all (mad).

So then I fought him.

I knocked him all out in the street.

So he say he give and I kept on hitting him.

Then he started crying and ran home to his father.

And the father told him that he didn't find no glove.

As William Labov remarks, the difference between the two is that the second has a consistent evaluative perspective or narrative line—from the speaker to the events that impinge upon him and back to his reactions to these events.[7]

A study by T.E. Strandberg and J. Griffith provides another example.[8] Four- and five-year-olds were given Kodak Instamatic cameras and told to take any pictures that interested them. Their subsequent utterances about these pictures were compared with what they said of comparable pictures that they had photographed when told to do so in order to learn. In the first of the two excerpts, the child struggles—unsuccessfully—to find a context for an assigned picture. In the second, describing one he took on his own, it is built in. The speaker is a five-year-old:

That's a horse. You can ride it. I don't know any more
about it. It's brown, black, and red. I don't know my
story about the horse.

There's a picture of my tree that I climb in.
There's—there's where it grows at and there's where I
climb up—and sit up there—down there and that's
where I look out at.
First I get on this one and then I get on that other one.
And then I put my foot under that big branch that are
so strong.
And then I pull my face up and when I get a hold of a
branch up at that place—and then I look around.

The bare, schoolboyish organization of the first seems so
detached next to the intentional, active, egocentric perspective
of the second.

Let us shift now to much younger children—infants of four
to six weeks, studied at the Center for Cognitive Studies. In a
study conducted by Ilze Kalnins, infants controlled the focus of
a lively motion picture by sucking at different rates on a special
nipple.[9] In one condition, sucking at or faster than a prescribed
rate brought the moving picture into focus and kept it there.
In the other, sucking at this rate drove the picture out of focus
and kept it out. One group of infants started with sucking for
clarity and shifted to the suck-for-blur condition. The other
began with the suck-for-blur and shifted to the suck-for-clear
condition—though the two conditions were never presented
in the same session, nor, indeed, on the same visit to the center.

Note two crucial points about performance. The first is
that the infants respond immediately and appropriately to the
consequences produced by their sucking, the pauses averaging
about four seconds in suck-for-clear and about eight seconds
in suck-for-blur. As soon as the consequences of sucking alters,

the infant's response pattern shifts abruptly and appropriately. As a further feature of reacting to consequences in both conditions, the infant averts his gaze from the picture when it is out of focus (while sucking in the case of suck-for-blur and while pausing in the other case).

For those not acquainted with the data on infant learning, these findings may seem a trifle bizarre though otherwise quite to be expected. They are, in fact, rather unexpected in respect to the immediacy of the learning reported, particularly in the light of the painfully slow process of classical conditioning found in infants of comparable age by H. Papousek and Lewis P. Lipsitt.[10] Papousek's infants turned their heads one way or another *in response* to an environmental event, as did the babies in the Brown University experiments. Kalnins' babies were responding not to a stimulus *but to a change produced by their own act*, learning to store the information thus gained as an instrumental sequence involving their own action. Indeed, it may well be that a special type of recurring critical period is to be found in the few thousand milliseconds that follow upon a voluntarily initiated act. This is not the proper context in which to treat the matter in detail, yet it must be said emphatically that since the pioneer work of E. von Holst and H. Mittelstaedt, the role of intention has become increasingly central in biology and psychology.[11]

While we are still far from understanding the neural mechanisms of intentionality—variously called reafference, feed-forward, motor-to-sensory mechanism, corollary discharge, or "Sollwert"—there are a sufficient number of leads to suggest that the pursuit will pay off. One such lead is provided by R. Held and A.V. Hein, who first showed how crucial is the reafference output of "intentional" movement for adaptation learning.[12] In their now famous experiment with yoked kittens adapting to prismatically induced angular displacement in the visual field, one kitten actively walked about an environment, the other was passively transported in a gondola through an identical path. The former adapted to the prisms, the latter did not.

In a word, probably the first type of acquired representation of the world the child achieves is in the form of an egocentrically oriented action schema: a joint representation of action intended along with the consequences of that action—a matter to which Jean Piaget has devoted some of his most exquisite descriptions.[13]

But if one thinks of acquired egocentric orientation only as a phase out of which the child must grow en route to becoming operational and decentered, then a crucial point may be overlooked. In L.S. Vygotsky's terms, the stream of action and the stream of language begin to converge in the process of interacting with the world in just such an egocentric orientation.[14]

My colleague Patricia M. Greenfield notes, "Not only can people fail to realize goals, the environment can fail to provide a growth-promoting sequence for them. I should like to suggest that the goals set for the child by his caretakers and the relation of these to the child's available means is a critical factor in determining the rate and richness of cognitive growth in the early, formative years."[15] She goes on to comment that "if a mother believes her fate is controlled by external forces, that she does not control the means necessary to achieve her goals, what does this mean for her children?" The follow-up data from the Hess group's study of the relation between maternal variables and the development of intelligence (to which we shall turn shortly) shows that the more a mother feels externally controlled when her child is four years old, the more likely the child is to have a low IQ and a poor academic record at the age of six or seven.[16]

Striking documentation of these points is beginning to be available at the intimate level of family interaction. One such study by Maxine Schoggen is an effort to elucidate differences in directed action that had been found in the children of the five-year study of Rupert A. Klaus and Susan W. Gray.[17] Schoggen uses an "environmental force unit," or EFU, which is defined as an act by any social agent in the child's environment directed toward getting the child to seek a goal. One crude finding already available (the data are now being analyzed) is that for lower-income families some two-thirds of the children are below the total median rate for EFU's per minute, whereas only a quarter of the middle-income children are. This suggests how great a difference there may be in sheer emphasis upon goal directedness in the two groups.

One must note also that a comparable trend emerged in the two major studies of how middle-class and poverty mothers instruct their children. These studies, one by Robert D. Hess and Virginia C. Shipman and the second by Helen L. Bee and others,[18] show that middle-class mothers are more attentive to the continuous flow of goal-directed action; allow the child to set his own pace and make his own decisions more; intrude less often and less directly in the process of problem solving itself; structure the search task by questions that sharpen yet ease the search for means; are more oriented toward the over-all structure of the task than responsive to component acts in isolation; and, finally, react more to (or reinforce) the child's successful efforts than his errors (a practice far more likely to evoke further verbal interaction between tutor and child). These surely suggest some of the crucial differences that emerge in the goal-seeking patterns of economically advantaged and disadvantaged children.

To this evidence must now be added still another type of research finding, resulting from longer-term longitudinal studies tracing human growth from infancy through adolescence.

Jerome Kagan and Howard A. Moss state in their well-known monograph, "It appears that the pattern most likely to lead to involvement in intellectual achievement in the boys is early maternal protection, followed by encouragement and acceleration of mastery behaviors."[19] And then, "Following our best judgment in estimating the most desirable patterns to follow with young children, our educated guess remains that higher intelligence is fostered by warmth, support, and plentiful opportunity and reward for achievement and autonomy. Moreover, it is probably important to provide active, warm, achievement-oriented parental figures of both sexes after whom appropriate role patterns can be established." Add to this, finally, the conclusion reached by H.B. Robinson and N.M. Robinson: "Children with a high degree of achievement motivation tend to become brighter as they grow older; those with a more passive outlook tend to fall behind their developmental potential. The degree of achievement motivation is related to the sociocultural background of the child; middle-class children are more strongly motivated toward achievement than are lower-class children."[20]

There is a further multiplier factor in the effects we have been discussing; that is, the impact of urbanization on the care of children. Until now we have argued that poverty, by its production of a sense of powerlessness, alters goal striving and problem solving in those it affects, whether the powerlessness occurs in a depressed London working-class borough, in a black ghetto, or in the midst of Appalachia; among Kurdistani immigrants to Israel, or among uneducated and abandoned Eskimo mothers from Greenland, down and out in literate Copenhagen. The evidence points to a magnification of this effect when the rural poor move to the city.

Perhaps the most comprehensive study to date is by Nancy B. Graves, who has compared rural and urban Spanish-Americans around Denver, as well as rural and urban Baganda around Kampala and Entebbe in Uganda.[21] Interviews with mothers in this study show that urban mothers come to believe more than rural mothers that their preschool children cannot understand, cannot be taught ideas or skills, cannot be depended upon. City mothers rated their children lower in potentialities for independence, self-reliance, and ability to help with the family. It is a cycle. When the poor mother moves to the city, she becomes trapped with her children; she becomes more irritable, more interested in keeping peace than in explaining and encouraging adventure, often producing the very behavior she rates down. At the same time that the urban environment itself restricts outlets for the child, it also reduces the mother's confidence in her children's capacity for coping with those outlets that are left.

In a masterful review of the literature on the effects of poverty, Warren Haggstrom comes to this conclusion: "The fact of being powerless, but with needs that must be met, leads the poor to be dependent on the organizations, persons, and institutions which can meet these needs. The situation of dependency and powerlessness, through internal personality characteristics as well as through social position, leads to apathy, hopelessness, conviction of the inability to act successfully, failure to develop skills, and so on."[22]

Let us consider now some consequences of this pattern on the development of language usage in interactive speech, together with some consequences that are likely to occur in the internal use of speech in problem solving.

Language and Poverty

It was perhaps the studies of Hess and Shipman inspired by Basil Bernstein, that drew attention to *how* language was used in communicating with young children and *what* its significance was to the lower- and the middle-class child.[23] They asked mothers to instruct their own children to use Etch-a-Sketch drawing pads, taking careful note of the mothers' language and mode of instruction. Their general conclusions have already been discussed. Looking in detail at linguistic considerations, we turn to a more recent study that used the Hess and Shipman system of classification with further elaboration. It documents the work carried out by Helen Bee and her colleagues at the University of Washington with four- to five-year-olds.[24] This university group also asked each mother to help her child accomplish a task (copying a house of blocks); in addition they observed mother-child interaction in the well-supplied waiting room and interviewed the mother afterwards about her ideas on looking after children. An excerpt from their paper can serve as summary:

> The middle-class mother tended to allow her child to work at his own pace, offered many general structuring suggestions on how to search for the solution to a problem, and told the child what he was doing that was correct . . .. The general structure offered by the mother may help the child acquire learning sets (strategies) which will generalize to future problem-solving situations.
>
> In contrast, the lower-class mother did not behave in ways which would encourage the child to attend to the basic features of the problem. Her suggestions were highly specific, did not emphasize basic problem-solving strategies, and seldom required reply from the child. Indeed, she often deprived the child of the opportunity to solve the problem on his own by her non-verbal intrusions into the problem-solving activity.

They comment on the fact that middle-class mothers ask so many more questions in an effort to help the child in his task, that their mode of operating linguistically could fairly be called interrogative in contrast to the more indicative and imperative modes of lower-class mothers.

Hess and Shipman, of course, had found quite comparable differences in mothers, though they distinguished three modes of communicating: cognitive-rational, imperative-normative, and personal-subjective. In the first mode, the mother was task-oriented, informative, and analytic; in the second, she ordered and evaluated; in the third, she pleaded for performance on grounds that it would please her. The highest concentration of the first mode was found among middle-class mothers.[25]

Both studies point to early class differences in language use. One is the use of language to dissect a problem. In lower-class discourse, mothers more often order, or plead, or complain, than set up a problem or give feedback. Such usage possibly accounts for the poor reinforcement value of verbal reactions by the parents of less-advantaged children, such as that described by E. Zigler and E. Butterfield; language is not usually used for signalling outcome or hailing good tries.[26] What is most lacking in the less-advantaged mother's use of language is analysis and synthesis: the dissection of relevant features in a task and their appropriate recombinings in terms of connection, cause and effect, and so on.

The evidence surely leads one to the conclusion that there is both more demand for and more use of analytic language among middle-class than among lower-class speakers. G. J. Turner and R. E. Pickvance, for example, attempted to measure the difference by counting incidences of uncertainty in the verbal expressions of sixteen-year-olds from middle-class and poverty backgrounds who were making up stories or interpreting uncertain events.[27] "Orientation toward the use of expressions of uncertainty is more strongly related to social class than to verbal ability . . .. In every case in which social class has been shown to be related to the use of expressions of uncertainty, it was the middle-class child who used more of them . . .." The middle-class child had more recourse to Wh-questions and to the use of "might be" or "could be" or "I think," and to a refusal to commit himself. As the authors observe, "Bernstein's work suggests that the forms of socialisation typically employed in middle-class families are likely to give the children reared in these families greater scope for self-regulation, for operating within a wide range of alternatives. These socialisation procedures . . . are likely to give these children a greater awareness of uncertainty in certain areas of experience and are likely to encourage the children to be flexible in their thinking."

Other evidence also suggests a difference in analytic discrimination. There is agreement in the findings of Rupert A. Klaus and Susan W. Gray, from studies of impoverished black children in Murfreesboro, Tennessee, and of W. P. Robinson and C. D. Creed, from studies of slum children in London's Borough of Newham, that less fine discriminations are made by lower-class than by middle-class children—at least in rather impersonal, school-like tasks.[28] Marion Blank and Frances Solomon show that tutoring children from poverty backgrounds to extract features from displays—distance, direction and form, for example—increases their measured intelligence (long a belief of Maria Montessori).[29] Indeed, it is not surprising that Earl S. Schaefer's careful intervention study with one- to three-year-old children in poverty familes emphasizes such discriminative training, with good results in raising standard intelligence scores.[30]

Another index of the analytic use of language is the accumulation of vocabulary. As C. B. Cazden puts it, "Consideration of vocabulary as an aspect of language cannot be separated from considerations of concepts as the whole of our personal knowledge. The content of our mental dictionary catalogs more than our knowledge of language; it catalogs our substantive knowledge of the world."[31] R. Brown, C. B. Cazden, and U. Bellugi also point out that most instances of natural language instruction between parent and child relate to word meanings—true not only in their small Cambridge sample but also for two lower-class black mothers in a Great Lakes city, as described by V. M. Horner, and for mothers in Samoa, as described by D. I. Slobin.[32]

It is of special interest that James S. Coleman and others have noted that vocabulary subtests of an IQ test were more correlated with differences in quality of schools than were achievement tests in more formal school subjects such as arithmetic and reading.[33] This suggests that the push to analysis, differentiation, synthesis, and so on is accompanied by a push to achieve economy of means of representation in words. Again, the more active the intellectual push of the environment, the more the differentiation of concepts and of words, which are their markers. Hence the richer, better stocked vocabulary of the middle-class child.

Perhaps the most telling example of the middle-class child's greater facility in handling analysis and synthesis in speech comes from Joan Tough's study of two groups of three-year-olds, matched for IQ and about equal in verbal output, one of middle-, the other of working-class background.[34] Even at this age, middle-class children single out many more qualitative features of the environment to talk about and, indeed, also talk much more of such relations between them as cause and effect. So there is good reason to believe that there is an early start to the differentiating process; while children from one social class move toward a program of linguistic analysis and synthesis, the other group moves toward something else. The latter is described by Klaus and Gray in observing that "the children with whom we worked tended to have little categorizing ability except in affective terms; they were highly concrete and im-mediate in their approaches to objects and situations."[35] Bern-stein also comments on the fact that in carrying on a role-play type of conversation of the he said/she said variety, the child from the slum area is often richer and less hesitant in his speech, as if the more direct and concrete affective tone of human inter-action were the preferred mode.[36] Perhaps the "something else" is more thematic, personal, and concrete.

Let me then suggest a tentative conclusion from the first part of this all too brief survey of class differences in language use. With Jacqueline J. Goodnow, and George A. Austin, I drew a distinction between *affective, functional,* and *formal* categories.[37] Affective categories involve the organization of events in terms of the immediate reactions they produce in the beholder, particular affect-laden reactions. Functional cate-gories are groupings of objects and events in terms of fitness for the achievement of some particular goal or the carrying out of a particular task. Formal categories are those governed by a set of relatively universal criterial attributes in terms of which things can be placed without reference either to their use or to the gut reaction they produce.

Although I am aware of how very insufficient the data still are, it would seem to be the case that middle-class upbringing has the tendency to push the child toward a habitual use of formal categories and strategies appropriate to such categorizing; such as, analysis of tasks, consideration of alternative possibilities, questioning and hypothesizing, and elaborating. It is a mode in which one uses language in a characteristic way: by constructing linguistically an analytic replica independent of the situation and its functional demands and manipulating the replica by the rules of language.

But note that it is not that children of different classes differ either in the amount of language that they command, nor in the variant rules that govern their language. Cazden and Labov have compiled enough evidence from the extant literature to cast serious doubt on both the "less" language and the "different" language theories of class difference.[38] The critical issue seems to be language *use* in a variety of situations and the manner in which home and subculture affects such usage. Or as D. Hymes puts it, children not only learn to form and interpret sentences but "also acquire knowledge of a set of ways in which sentences are used."[39]

A striking experiment by E. R. Heider, C. B. Cazden, and R. Brown remind us again that the lower-class child, under appropriate conditions, *can* operate analytically quite well, though he might ordinarily or habitually not do so.[40] Heider and his collaborators asked lower-class and middle-class ten-year-old boys to describe a picture of an animal in a fashion that would later permit distinguishing it from many other similar pictures. Some of the attributes the boys used in their descriptions were criterial in the sense of defining uniquely the target or reducing materially the range of possiblities; others were irrelevant for guiding one to the correct target. Both groups of boys mentioned roughly the same total number of attributes. Moreover, both groups mentioned about the same number of criterial attributes: 18 out of a total of 67 for middle-class boys, 16 out of 69 for the other group. Where the two groups differed was in the number of adult prompts and requests that were necessary to draw the attributes out of them: an average of 6.11 for the lower-class children and only 3.56 for the middle-class group. By the same token, Francis Palmer finds that if seven or eight hours are spent prior to testing in establishing an easy rapport between the adults and the children, most differences between lower-class and middle-class children become minimal.[41] This point was also established by Labov when he concluded that the language usage of northern blacks does not differ structurally or in underlying logic from standard English.[42]

What seems to be at issue again is the question of "personalness" and the egocentric axis. If the situation is personal and egocentrically organized, then the lower-class child can be just as complex as the middle-class one. But the lower-class child seems far less able to analyze things in the world from a perspective other than his personal or local perspective. Perhaps this point will become more compelling when we examine a second feature of language that differentiates between social classes, to which we turn now. This second feature involves communicating through language in a fashion independent of the situation.

Grace de Laguna says, "The evolution of language is characterized by a progressive freeing of speech from dependence on the perceived conditions under which it is uttered and heard, and from the behavior which accompanies it."[43] She argues that the superior power of a written language inheres in this freedom from the contexts of action and perception; to use the familiar contemporary term of Jerrold J. Katz and Jerry A. Fodor, all of the "semantic markers" of a written language are inherent in the utterance itself—they are "intrasemantic" rather than "extrasemantic."[44]

Greenfield remarks on how the speech of technologically oriented societies (in contrast to preliterate, more traditionally oriented ones) becomes more like a written language in its increasing independence from context. The title of her paper, "On Speaking a Written Language," is apposite not only, I think, to the trend in spoken language from a preliterate to a literate society, but also from working-class to middle-class society in Western culture.[45] Bernstein provides an interesting reason for the class difference.

> We can see that the class system has affected the distribution of knowledge. Historically and now, only a tiny proportion of the population has been socialized into knowledge at the level of the metalanguages of control and innovation, whereas the mass of population has been socialized into knowledge at the level of context-tied operations . . . .. This suggests that we might be able to distinguish between two orders of meaning. One we would call universalistic, the other particularistic. Universalistic meanings are those in which principles and operations are made linguistically explicit, whereas particularistic orders of meaning are meanings in which principles and operations are relatively linguistically implicit. If orders of meaning are universalistic, then the meanings are less tied to a given context. The metalanguage of public forms of thought as these apply to objects and persons realize meanings of a universalistic type. Where meanings have this characteristic, then individuals have access to the grounds of their experience and can change the grounds. . . . Where the meaning system is particularistic, much of the meaning is imbedded in the context of the social relationship. In this sense the meanings are tied to a context and may be restricted to those who share a similar contextual history. Where meanings are universalistic, they

are in principle available to all, because the principles and operations have been made explicit and so public. I shall argue that forms of socialization orient the child toward speech codes which control access to relatively context-tied or relatively context-independent meanings.[46]

In short, it is the parochializing effect of a culture of poverty that keeps language tied to context, tied to common experience, restricted to the habitual ways of one's own group. This comparative dependence on context of the language of disadvantaged children shows up early. In Tough's work on three- to four-year-olds from middle- and lower-class backgrounds in an English industrial city, the children were matched on Stanford-Binet scores and, roughly, on verbal output.[47] Here are Tough's findings, as related by P. R. Hawkins:

> All of the children's "items of representation" . . . were rated as to whether they required the presence of the concrete situation for effective communication. This concrete component constitutes 20.9 per cent of the representation of the favoured children and 34.5 per cent of the less favoured children. The most frequent form of the concrete component are pronouns whose only reference is to something pointed at in the environment. Such "exophoric" reference is contrasted with "anaphoric" reference, where pronouns refer to an antecedent previously supplied in words. The percentage of anaphoric references was 22.8 per cent for the favoured children and only 7.7 per cent for the less favoured. This finding replicated Bernstein's research with children five to seven years old.[48]

I do not know, save by everyday observation, whether the difference is greater still among adults, but my impression is that the difference in decontextualization is greater between an English barrister and a dock worker than it is between their children.

Two trends, then, seem to be operative in the use of language by middle-class children. One is the use of language as an instrument of analysis and synthesis in problem solving wherein the analytic power of language aid (in abstraction or feature extraction) and the generative, transformational powers of language are used in reorganizing and synthesizing the features thus abstracted. The second trend is toward decontextualization, toward learning to use language without dependence upon shared percepts or actions, with sole reliance on the linguistic self-sufficiency of the message. Decontextualization permits information to be conceived as independent of the speaker's vantage point. It permits communications with those who do not share one's daily experience or actions, and in fact, as Bernstein insists, allows one to transcend restrictions of locale and affiliation.[49] Lower-class language, in contrast, is more affective and metaphoric than formal or analytic in its use, more given to narrative then to causal or generic form. It is more tied to place and affiliation, serving the interests of concrete familiarity rather than generality, more tied to finding than to seeking.

Both trends seem to reflect the kind of goal-striving and problem-solving characteristic of those who have accepted without protest occupancy of the bottom roles and statuses in the society that roughly constitute the position of poverty. It is not merely that the poor are "victims" of the system—they are indeed, but so is everybody else in some way. It is rather that a set of values, a way of goal seeking, a way of dealing with means and ends becomes associated with poverty.

Social Reciprocity

Being socioeconomically disadvantaged is no simple matter of suffering a cultural avitaminosis that can be dosed by suitable inputs of vitamins in the form of compensatory experiences. It is a complex of circumstances at the center of which is usually a family whose wage earner is without a job or where there is no male wage earner. If there is a job, it usually is as demeaning in status as it is unremunerative. The setting is a neighborhood that has adapted itself often with much human bravura to being at the bottom, with little by way of long-range perspective or hope, often alienated by a sense of ethnic separation from the main culture.

This is not the place to examine the economic, social, and political means whereby some societies segregate social classes by restricting access to knowledge and eroding in childhood the skills needed to gain and use knowledge. The techniques of segregation by class are not deliberately planned, and they often resist deliberate efforts at abolition. More to the point is to ask how the behavior patterns of the dispossessed are transmitted by the family to produce the forms of coping associated with poverty.

We have already encountered a striking difference in the use of reward and punishment by the mother. One finding by Bee and her colleagues suggests that the transmission may be accomplished by so simple a factor as rewarding achievement in the middle class while punishing or ridiculing failure among children of the poor. Several studies point to a by-product in the form of a class difference in asking adults for help, as described by L. Kohlberg, in showing doubt in their presence, as discussed by P. R. Hawkins.[50] The poor do much less of both.

Modelling of class patterns by adults—both in interaction with the child and in general—may be another source of family transmission. D. Hamburg draws some interesting inferences about such modelling from studies of higher primates.[51] He writes, "The newer field studies suggest the adaptive significance of observational learning in a social context. Time and again, one observes the following sequence: (1) close observation of one animal by another; (2) imitation by the observing animal of the behavior of some observed animal; and (3) the later practice of the observed behavior, particularly in the play group of young animals." A like point is made for preliterate people, as in the close study of Talensi education and play by

Meyer Fortes and the detailed observation of children's play among the Bushmen by Lorna Marshall.[52] They, too, point to the conclusion that observation and imitative incorporation in play is widespread and seemingly central.

Early language acquisition seems almost to be the type case of modelling. In a recent and detailed review of the language acquisition of the children being studied at Harvard University by Brown, Cazden, and Bellugi, the importance of modelling is highlighted. But this work suggests that modelling is not a simple form of transmission.

The puzzling and challenging thing about learning language from a model is that the child is not so much copying specific language behavior from observation and imitation, but rather is developing general rules about how to behave from which various specific acts can be appropriately derived or interpreted. It is not at all clear how much we should attribute in early learning to the reinforcing effects of reward and punishment and how much to such rule learning acquired by observing or interacting with a model. Discussing the role of approval and disapproval as possible influences in the acquisition of grammar, Brown and his colleagues say,

> In general, the parents fitted propositions to the child's utterances, however incomplete or distorted the utterances, and then approved or not according to the correspondence between proposition and reality. Thus, "Her curl my hair" was approved because the mother was in fact curling Eve's hair. However, Sarah's grammatically impeccable "There's the animal farmhouse" was disapproved because the building was a lighthouse . . .. It seems then to be truth value rather than syntactic well formedness that chiefly governs explicit verbal reinforcement by parents— which renders mildly paradoxical the fact that the usual product of such a training schedule is an adult whose speech is highly grammatical but not notably truthful.[53]

If it turns out to be the case that the young child is learning not only linguisitic rules but also rules about roles and rules about ways of thinking and ways of talking, then indoctrination in class patterns must be, in the linguist's sense, generative and pervasive to a degree that is difficult to estimate. This would make even more meaningful the insistence of Sarah Smilansky that intervention programs emphasize rationale and explanation in order to reach the deep conceptual level where the class pattern rules operate.[54] In sum, both through the compelling effects of approval and disapproval and by the modelling of rule-bound behavior, the family passes on class patterns of goal striving, problem solving, paying attention, and so forth.

In closing this section, let me make one thing clear. I am *not* arguing that middle-class culture is good for all or even good for the middle class. Indeed, its denial of the problems of dispossession, poverty, and privilege make it contemptible in the eyes of even compassionate critics. Nor do I argue that the culture of the dispossessed is not rich and varied within its limits. There are critics, like S. S. and J. C. Baratz, who are too ready to cry racist to what they sense to be derogation of black culture, or Yemeni culture, or Cockney culture.[55] But insofar as a subculture represents a reaction to defeat and insofar as it is caught by a sense of powerlessness, it suppresses the potential of those who grow up under its sway by discouraging problem solving. The source of powerlessness that such a subculture generates, no matter how moving its by-products, produces instability in the society and unfulfilled promise in human beings.

Culture and Theories of Development

Thus far we have concentrated upon how a culture of poverty reflects itself in child rearing. But there is no reason to believe that the effects of such child rearing are either inevitable or irreversible—there are ways of altering the impact of middle-class pressures or of poverty. In order to appreciate better this likelihood of change, we must look briefly at the nature of human development and at theories designed to explicate it.

There is a paradox in contemporary formulations. We have, on the one hand, rejected the idea of culture-free intelligence, and probably the Coleman report put the finishing blow to the idea of school-free tests of intelligence.[56] In this view, intelligence depends on the incorporation of culture. At the same time, there is a current vogue for theories of intellectual development that sustain education strategies which presumably are unaffected, or virtually unaffected, by class difference, cultural background, and other conditions of the life of the child—short, perhaps, of pathology. According to such theories, the only differences lie in the timing, the steps being the same. It is a matter only of slower and faster, not of difference in kind. So on the one side we urge a context-sensitive view, while on the other we propose that intelligence grows from the inside out, with support from the environment being only in the form of nourishment appropriate to the stage of development— a relatively context-free conception formulated most comprehensively by Piaget's Geneva school.[57]

I suspect both kinds of theory are necessary—at least they have always existed. The strength of a context-free view is that it searches for universal structures of mind; its weakness is its intrinsic anticulturalism. H. Aebli notes the Geneva dilemma: if the child only takes in what he is ready to assimilate, why bother to teach before he is ready, and since he takes it in naturally once he is ready, why bother afterwards?[58] On the other hand, the weakness of most context-sensitive views of development is that they give too much importance to individual and cultural differences and overlook the universals of growth. Their strength, of course, is in a sensitivity to the nature of the human plight and how this plight is fashioned by culture.

Two things, it seems to me, can keep us mindful of both universality and cultural diversity. The first is an appreciation of the universals of human culture, which revolve most often around reciprocal exchange through symbolic, affiliative, and economic systems. To alter man's participation in any of these systems of exchange is to force a change in how man carries out the enterprises of life. For what must be adjusted to is precisely these exchange systems—what we come to expect by way of respect, affiliation, and goods. Herein is where poverty is so crucial an issue—for poverty in economic life affects family structure, one's symbolic sense of worth, and one's feeling of control.

But beyond the universals of culture, there are universals in man's primate heritage. The primate progression illustrates to an extraordinary degree the emergence of curiosity, play, anticipation, and, ultimately, the human species' characteristic ways of seeking, transforming, representing, and using information. Our review thus far has surely shown us how hope, confidence, and a sense of the future can affect the unfolding and nurturing of these capacities. If the conditions imposed by a culture can alter hopes and shrink confidence, it can surely alter the use of these species-typical patterns of behavior. Theories of development are guides for understanding the perfectibility of man as well as his vulnerability. They define man's place in nature and identify the signal opportunities that exist for improving or changing his lot by aiding growth. A theory of development that specifies nothing about intervention is blind to culture; one that specifies only intervention is blind to man's biological inheritance.

On Intervention

With respect to virtually any criterion of equal opportunity and equal access to opportunity, the children of the poor—particularly the urban poor—are plainly not getting as much schooling, or as much from it, as their middle-class peers. By any conservative estimate of what happens before school, about a half million of the roughly 4 million children of each year of age in the United States are receiving substandard fare in day care, nursery school, kindergarten, guidance, and so forth. This is not intended to be a psychological assessment but a description of resources, i.e., officially agreed-upon facilities.[59]

A few typical figures illustrate the point. The kindergarten population in the United States in 1966 was 3 million out of approximately 12 million of the age group from three through five; and the chances of a child in the lowest quarter bracket of the national income being in kindergarten were immeasurably less than of a child in the top quarter. In 1967, there were 193,000 children in full-year Head Start, a definite improvement but a fraction of the estimated 20 per cent of the 8 million three- and four-year-olds who needed it, or 1 million. One should note that more than 80 per cent of parents covered in one study said that their children improved as a result of Head Start, a fact to be reckoned with in the light of the Rosenthal effect and Graves' findings on the ebbing confidence of poor urban mothers in their children.[60] Finally, in 1968 there were some 2.2 million working mothers in America with children three to five; many of these mothers were the sole breadwinner in the family. In that same year, there were approximately 310,000 places for children in registered day-care centers and in approved private-home arrangements, one place per seven mothers. The 1970 estimate is that 9 per cent of children two to five years of age and 14 per cent of children three to five with working mothers are enrolled in day care.

I have been expressing the view that induction into this so-called culture of failure begins early. In New York and other cities, half the children born in poverty are illegitimate. Growing up in an urban ghetto—influenced by the family structure it often produces and the neighborhoods and schools it spawns—surely diminishes the skills and confidence needed to use the benefits of modern industrial, democratic society on one's own behalf or on behalf of one's own group. Romanticism about poverty and its effects on growth is middle-class escapism.

Probably we cannot change this plight without changing the society that permits such poverty to exist during a time of affluence. My first recommendation, as a commonsense psychologist and as a concerned man, would be that we should transform radically the structure of our society. But that is not our topic. What can one do now within the context of the changing society of today?

In preparing a summary of reports on major programs of intervention at a symposium on the "Education of the Infant and Young Child," held by the American Association for the Advancement of Science late in 1969, I was struck by the broad agreement on several significant points.

First, whatever the program, enormous influence is exerted by the mother, the child's day-to-day caretaker. She is a major factor in any program; one must work with her, not merely compensate for her.

Second, growth involves small, step-by-step increments in the acquisition of skill and competence on a day-to-day basis. Though theories of development emphasize principally the great leaps forward, it is in the management of daily progress that discouragement or encouragement occurs, where progress can be shaped in one direction or another.

Third, there is an enormous contribution to cognitive development from factors that on the surface are anything but traditionally cognitive—such diffuse affective factors as confidence, the capacity to control one's environment, and hope in the future. These likewise are affected by daily events, and they reflect as well the mother's mood.

Fourth, the concept of enrichment tends to put the child in the position of a passive consumer. One study after another shows that if he is to benefit, the child must be helped to be on his own—to operate eventually on his own activation. It is this that must be cultivated and supported.

Fifth, and very practically, there seem to be a wide range of alternative ways to succeed in an intervention program—provided only that they produce opportunities for mother and child to carry out activities that have some kind of structure.

Beyond these specific conclusions, a general one stood out: the importance of initiative in the community as a means of activating parents and caretakers to do something for their children.

Haggstrom again makes telling points in discussing the power of the poor.[61]

In order to reduce poverty-related psychological and social problems in the United States, the major community will have to change its relationship to neighborhoods of poverty in such a fashion that families in the neighborhoods have a greater stake in the broader society and can more successfully participate in the decision-making process . . .. The poor must as a group be helped to secure opportunities for themselves. Only then will motivation be released that is now locked in the silent and usually successful battle of the neighborhoods of poverty to maintain themselves in an alien social world. This motivation . . . will enable them to enter the majority society and make it as nurturant of them as it is at present of the more prosperous . . .. One way in which the poor can remedy the psychological consequences of their powerlessness and of the image of the poor as worthless is for them to undertake social action that redefines them . . ..

Haggstrom identifies five conditions that he believes must be present if such social action is to be effective:

1. The poor must see themselves as the source of the action.

2. The action must affect in major ways the preconceptions, values, or interests of the poor.

3. The action must make demands in terms of putting forth effort and utilizing skills.

4. The action must end in success.

5. The successful self-originated important action must be seen as enhancing the symbolic value of specific people who are poor.

Haggstrom's list is admittedly ambitious. Even so, it falls short of dealing with some intractable correlates of poverty, as race in the case of the American black, as nationality with the Italian-Swiss, and so on. Yet it surely provides a sense of the role of community action in providing a background for countering the very problems of goal seeking, problem solving, and language usage we have been discussing.

Granted the importance of community action and revolutionary aspirations in the struggle against poverty's effects, one can still discuss psychological help for the child of poverty so that he may grow more effectively, not just into a middle-class suburban child (who has problems of his own) but rather into one capable of helping himself and his own community more effectively. It is with some considerations along these lines that I should like to end this chapter.

The expression "no room at the bottom" means something. With an increase in technological complexity, capital-intensive rather than labor-intensive techniques come to prevail. Instead of more labor to run the economy, more intensively skilled labor is used. While school rejects can be absorbed in a society built on stoop-labor, they can no longer find a place in a society where even the street sweeper is giving way to well-designed, motorized brushing machines. Since the first steps toward dropping out take place at home, the home is where the first remedies must be applied—merely the first, for it avails little to give help in the nursery only to defeat the child later in school.

The objective of curricula for young children, as for older ones, is to produce the kind of generalist in skill—the skill-intensive worker—who is capable of acting as a controlling factor in the regulating, running, or curbing of a technology such as we are developing in the West; or one who is capable of understanding it well enough to serve, to criticize, to be controller rather than victim. To put it plainly, I am assuming that man's cultural and biological evolution is toward general skill and intelligence and that the major difficulty we face is not in achieving such skill but in devising a society that can use it wisely. This means a society in which man feels at home and fulfilled enough to strive and to use his gifts. I am taking for granted that we do *not* want to curb idiosyncrasy, surprise, and the inevitable stridency that go with freedom.

My colleagues at the Center for Cognitive Studies, Patricia Greenfield and Edward Tronick, have been devising a curriculum for a day-care center at Bromley Heath in the Roxbury section of Boston. I have been enormously impressed with a set of implicit principles underlying their work—principles that I have extracted from one of their memoranda, but with which they may not agree. Nevertheless, let me run through them briefly, not with a view toward comprehensiveness but toward illustration. There are many echoes here from earlier sections of this chapter.

The active organism. Human intelligence is active and seeking. It needs an environment to encourage such action.

Effort after meaning. The search for meaning and regularity begins at birth. There is a constant search for cues for significance that needs nurturing.

Intentionality. Action and the search for meaning are guided by intention, self-directed, and help can be provided to sustain such self-direction.

Pace. Each age and activity have a pace that requires respect and patience from those around the baby.

Receptivity and state. There is a state of alert, awake receptivity when the child is hospitable to the environment. Use it for getting to the infant, rather than trying to break through unreceptive states.

Cycles of competence. Each newly emerging skill has a cycle of competence: initial crude effort, followed by consolidation and perfecting, followed by a period of variation. The phases require recognition to be helped to their completion.

Prerequisites. Skills require prior skills for mastery, as for example the fail-safe method of sitting down from a standing position before risking walking. Opportunity to master prerequisites helps later skills.

Appropriateness of play and objects. Different activities have requirements that can be met by providing appropriate games, play, or objects. The child intent on exploring small irregularities with his fingers will work for hours on a board with irregular holes cut in it, each differently colored.

Principles of the enterprise. Activity, as the child grows older, is more temporally organized under the control of intention. It is dependent upon mobilizing means to achieve an objective. Provision of means and encouragement for such enterprises and protection from distraction is of utmost importance to growth.

Principle of representation. Useful memory depends upon finding effective ways of representing information—be it in customary action, in a well-liked game, in a vivid picture, or in words. Marking something for later use or recognition is an important aspect of growth.

Analysis and synthesis. Problem solving often consists of reducing a task or situation to its component parts and then reorganizing them. Taking apart and putting together games, objects, stories, problems, is practice for such activity.

Time perspective. The future is constructed by each human being by coming to expect, by planning and achieving planned objectives, by doing one thing so one may do the next, by learning how to hope and anticipate with realistic confidence. The process is long and begins early—probably with peek-a-boo.

Principle of attachment. Human young, perhaps more than any other, are dependent on a consistent caretaker who is there with warmth, certainty, and effectiveness. It is in interaction with a caretaker that much of earliest learning occurs.

A well-informed, decently satisfied, and hopeful caretaker is worth a pound of cure.

In summary, persistent poverty over generations creates a culture of survival. Goals are short-range, restricted. The outsider and the external world are suspect. One stays inside and gets what one can. Beating the system takes the place of using the system.

Such a culture of poverty gets to the young early, influencing the way they learn to set goals, mobilize means, delay or fail to delay gratification. Very early, too, they learn in-group talk and thinking; just as their language use reflects less long-range goal analysis, it also tends toward a parochialism that makes it increasingly difficult to move or work outside the poverty neighborhood and the group. Make no mistake about it: it is a rich culture, intensely personalized and full of immediate rather than remote concerns. The issue is certainly not cultural deprivation, to be handled with a massive dose of compensatory enrichment.

Rather the issue is to make it possible for the poor to gain a sense of their own power through jobs, through community activation, through creating a sense of projection into the future. Jobs, community action under community control, a decent revision of preschool and early school opportunities—all of these are crucial. But just as crucial is a sense of the change in the times: the insistence of the powerless that their plight is not a visitation of fate, but a remediable condition. If we cannot produce that kind of change, then our system—which has worked fairly well, if exploitatively, since the industrial revolution—will doubtless collapse, probably to be replaced by something premised far more on coercion for all rather than just for some. That is why the generation to be raised is so crucial a resource. It may be our last chance.

3. The Crucible of the Urban Classroom

Staten W. Webster

If one asks what is the most serious defect of the urban school, the most valid reply is simply that it has not been able to adjust to change. Most urban schools are still organized as they were twenty years ago and still function as they did then despite the great changes that have taken place in the world around them.

Eager, highly motivated, middle-class youngsters disappear from the populations of the schools of the inner city only to turn up in private or suburban schools. Teachers acclimatized to instructional situations that were peaceful and rewarding now face numbers of students who are different in physical appearance from their former students, and who not only are less docile and compliant but also less willing to pursue the typical goals touted by the schools. The low levels of aspiration, motivation, and achievement found increasingly in many central-city schools are sources of great frustration for educators. It is too often forgotten that teachers need to experience feelings of success and accomplishment, as do all human beings.

Many experienced teachers cannot cope with the culture-shock of a school and its community that is shifting both in ethnic composition and social class. These instructors select less stressful settings. Newcomers to the profession are rushed like basic trainees into these demanding situations, often with

66

little or no special preparation. Their problems are compounded by the inflexibility and frequently the unwillingness of the urban school district to attempt divergent instructional and curricular strategies, even though present programs are failing.

This chapter is directed to a consideration of five key factors that contribute directly or indirectly to the crucible of the urban classroom.

In looking at problems of a teacher in a particular classroom, one is immediately aware that the school does not exist or operate in isolation from the influences of the broader society. The urban school and its teachers are the indirect targets of the fallout from social issues and conflicts present in the society at large. Riots, assassinations of public figures, and confrontations between citizens and police clearly have a strong impact upon what goes on in schools.

Therefore we must first examine how societal problems and issues spill over into the confines of the classroom itself. Problems of class and caste, the pressures of a complex and highly industrialized productive system, public dissatisfaction with the Vietnam War, high taxes, and other such problems— all these have their effect upon the educational process.

The key actors in the drama of the classroom are the students and their teachers. The journey from infancy to adulthood is marked by a series of developmental tasks that children and youths must master. Some youth-adult problems are the simple and even necessary products of this process of growing from infancy to adulthood, which is the second area explored in this chapter. This source of problems is too often overlooked when adults try to understand and deal with the behavior of children and youths.

The third factor considered is the impact of the socialization process and the role that is played by the values, standards, and attitudes of the homes from which the students come. Here we look at families representative of various social-class strata and ethnic groups.

Many of the problems faced by the teacher in the urban classroom clearly have their etiology in the nature of the organization and operation of the school as an institution. However, it is also true, unfortunately, that teachers as individuals contribute to the difficulties they face in today's urban classroom. The final sections of this chapter are therefore devoted to the behavior, attitudes, and concerns of teachers and the ways in which the school as an institution inhibits the learning process.

Social Change and the Schools

Arthur Pearl of the University of Oregon contends that America is increasingly becoming a "credential society." The significance of this concept is that almost any form of economically rewarding social activity will require, in the future, some form of degree, credential, certificate of completion, or license. Under such a system, educational attainment becomes the crucial ladder to success in the society. The reality of the coming credential society generates a great deal of concern, competition, and anxiety among the more upwardly mobile segment of the population regarding the educational success of their children. Among the groups that comprise the lower strata of the social-class hierarchy, a growing awareness of the significance of the credential society has the effect of increasing the despair, resignation, apathy, and overt hostility they already feel toward schools and the society. Meanwhile, some significant changes are taking place within the family as a social institution. These changes are also having an important impact on the role of the schools.

Edgar Z. Friedenberg contends that the American family today plays less of a role in the socialization of the young, because it has less of an effect upon the life chances of the young.[1] Earlier, when life was simpler and change less rapid, he argues, elders knew more that was useful than did their children. Children were more dependent upon their parents not only for what they learned but also for status and later economic security—or at least opportunity. A son today may never see his father at work; he may never see a single product of his parent's labor. The explosion in the amount of available knowledge and the growth of technology make it impossible for parents to tutor their children in all that they should know. Thus, the symbiotic tie that in earlier years existed between parent and child has been weakened. As Friedenberg states, " . . . the development of an open, bureaucratic society has weakened the influence of the family, and has transferred the task of distributing status among claimants primarily to the schools, which profess to judge them, so far as possible, without regard to their antecedents."[2]

There is also the vitally important and growing role of media. Today's children and youth are perhaps the best informed generation that this society has ever produced. It is perhaps correct that much of their information relates to contemporary events, and this is important. Most of the shortcomings and problems of the society are out in the open and accessible to all through television in particular, as well as through radio, the press, and motion pictures. Youngsters see poverty, wealth, violence, riots, and wars; they hear of corruption in high places; they become quickly aware of the many discrepancies in all facets of American life. A teenager cannot help but be influenced by seeing a documentary television program on hunger in the United States, after having seen another program dealing with some film or television star who is paid a million dollars for four summer spectaculars.

Regardless of race, ethnic status, or social class, today's youth are becoming increasingly uneasy about these inconsistencies in our society. They doubt the sincerity, the veracity, the commitments of adults. They are less willing to pursue the same goals as did earlier generations. More and more they question the relevance, the real social importance, of the subjects they are required to learn and to master in schools.

The so-called subculture of adolescents that has developed in this country is only to be found in modern, literate, highly industrialized societies that can afford to isolate or exclude its youth from full participation in the society. A growing sense of frustration in youth seems to be traceable to the fact that they are treated in a sense like second-class citizens. They are expected to act like adults, and yet society delays bestowing upon them all of the rights and privileges of such status. Friedenberg states thus the problems of contemporary youth:

> 'Youth culture' is composed of individuals whose time is preempted by compulsory school attendance or the threat of induction into the armed services, who, regardless of their skills, cannot get and hold jobs that will pay enough to permit them to marry and build homes, and who are subject to surveillance at home or in school dormitories if they are detected in any form of sexual activity whatever. Youth and prisoners are the only people in America for whom *all* forms of sexual behavior are defined as illicit. It is absurd to scrutinize people who are forced to live under such extraordinary disabilities for psychological explanations of their resistance or bizarre conduct, except insofar as their state of mind can be related to their real situation.[3]

Contributing to the problem is youth's inability to find truly significant things to do, which might offer the possibility of improving the human condition in society. Almost every summer job campaign for youth falls far short of its projected goals. A second problem results from the extent to which our society has commercialized and institutionalized the preadult period, so much so that it has become a distinct way of life with its own codes, mores, and artifacts.

At the same time that our society demands that youth be delayed in achieving adult status, we provide young people with far more freedom from adult domination and supervision and with greater mobility than any preceding generation has known. The problem is well put by Rudolf Dreikurs and Loren Grey:

> There appears little question that children today have more freedom than they did in the past; but freedom is not equality. Because children feel that they are denied genuine participation in the community, they refuse to accept the responsibilities that go with freedom. At the same time they demand more and more rights. Today's children feel that they have little to say in the decisions that affect their welfare; accordingly, they turn to the pursuit of pleasure as a means of compensating for this neglect.[4]

There is, of course, increasing concern in this country over law and order, the crime rate, and antisocial behavior by children as well as adults. Numerous theories have been advanced to explain antisocial or delinquent behavior by youth.

Richard A. Cloward and Lloyd E. Ohlin have offered a theory of delinquency that sees antisocial behavior as being the product of deprivation.[5] In other words, youths who live in a society that places a great deal of emphasis upon achievement and success, yet denies them the opportunity of attaining these goals, become deprived individuals. Certainly it is a barrier to success to be a member of a family trapped in the vicious cycle of poverty and to be, in addition, a member of a subordinate ethnic group. These authors contend that when youths are thus deprived of access to the usual channels of social success, they turn to deviant behavior. Such behavior is said to lead to three possible adaptations to frustrations. Youths can (1) engage in criminal activity to gain material and status goals; (2) react by engaging in conflict-type activity with those who are seen as a source of oppression; or (3) form retreatist subcultures that reject the traditional goals espoused by the society.

A greater portion of antisocial behavior is engaged in by the disadvantaged segment of our society. Charles V. Willie, however, feels that the deprivation-of-opportunity view of

Cloward and Ohlin is an over-simplification of the problem.[6] Willie contends that both segregation (class or ethnic) and related feelings of alienation operate to produce antisocial behavior. Carried to extremes, alienation can lead to acts of hostility and feelings of hate. This point of view is most relevant in the case of such ethnic groups as blacks, Puerto Ricans, poor whites, and Mexican-Americans.

Willie contends that adult society must bear much of the responsibility for the antisocial behavior of many youths.[7] First, adults refuse to accord acceptance to youths until they have proved their acceptability to adults. Second, society makes little or no real effort to win the confidence of youths, who counter by feeling that they cannot trust this kind of adult society; they then withhold their commitment to its rules and regulations and refuse to identify with its goals and values.

Central to the entire problem under discussion is the rapidly increasing proportion of nonwhites in the urban population and, moreover, the changing composition of this group. A growing segment of the black population has spent all of its life in central cities. They have never been exposed to the extremely oppressive conditions that their predecessors experienced in the South. Their view of life is modern and northern in its orientation. Such young blacks, as well as increasing numbers of Mexican-Americans and Puerto Ricans, are becoming painfully cognizant of their secondary status in the society, and they resent it.* Nationalist and militant movements have increased appeal to the young black. The growth of such movements can be attributed in part to a loss of faith by blacks and others in the ultimate success of the civil rights movement.

The growing demands of minorities for power and control over their own communities can be understood only if one

---

*A significant, and often overlooked fact about the newcomers to the city, is that they tend to have higher levels of educational attainment than the resident population.[8] One explanation for this phenomenon is that the inmigrants tend to be younger than the population that they are joining.

realizes that the legislative and legal victories achieved during the civil rights struggle between 1954 and 1966 touched the lives of less than 10 per cent of the blacks in this country and far fewer of the members of other ethnic minority groups. Of what value to a poor person is a public accommodations law if he can't afford the price of a room in a Hilton hotel? What is the direct consequence of equal opportunities in employment programs if one has no specific skill and limited educational attainment? The civil rights movement did little for the poor minority-group masses of the country.

If the foregoing factors are indeed the salient ones operative today in American society, what are some problems that they present to educators and the schools?

The development of the credential society, as described by Pearl, in itself is creating two kinds of problems. As the failure of the urban school to produce desired levels of achievement in pupils becomes more widely known, parents—especially low-income minority parents—generate considerable pressure on school personnel for improvements. It becomes increasingly difficult, for example, in many California black communities, for boards of education to assign nonblack administrators to schools in these areas. Meanwhile, in suburban communities and in middle-class dominated schools, pressure relating to the growing importance of education can result in excessive pressure on students and the overinvolvement of parents in the educational process.

The isolated status of adolescents in American society is productive of a natural degree of hostility between such youth and adults. Teachers who find themselves assigned to a custodial function by the society become the prime targets of the frustrations of youth. The nature of the educational establishment is such that teachers and schools generally operate to carry out the commands of the taxpaying public. Very few administrators or teachers have assumed the role of an advocate on behalf of youth when such support is needed.

The rapid nature by which information and ideas can be communicated is productive of large numbers of children and youths who seem geared to see much of reality in terms of *now*. Much of the content of the school curriculum relates to the past. Such content is often rejected by larger numbers of students as being irrelevant and unnecessary. It becomes much more difficult for teachers to help students become motivated to pursue the typical goals of the school. The recent awareness of the biased nature of the curriculum, as it relates to the history and accomplishments of minorities, leads to a greater rejection of the typical curriculum by some students and increased pressure by others for new curricula.

As numbers of nonwhites increase in central cities, the school populations reflect these changes. In a growing number of cities, nonwhite students either have or threaten to become the dominant group in the schools. Where this has happened, it has become increasingly difficult for schools to receive adequate financial support from the dominant (white) group that retains numerical supremacy in the city and control over its political and economic institutions. Funds for education in the central city become less available and both teachers and the educational services of the schools suffer.

The racial issue does not respect the sanctity of the classroom. White teachers, especially in the upper grades, feel the shock waves from this area of conflict in our society. Learning cannot take place when mutual respect, understanding, and compassion are absent in classrooms.

Maturation and Developmental Tasks

The growth process and developmental tasks accompanying it are all too often overlooked as potential sources of turbulence in classrooms. In examining this problem, we will begin with latency, the term often applied to the childhood period from six to eleven or twelve years of age.

There are some six developmental tasks that learners in the childhood group face.[9] The mastery of each of these tasks can be productive of problems for both parents and teachers. One of the first things that must be accomplished by a child moving from the often protective environment of the home and family to that of the school is the development of a certain sense of personal independence. In his new setting he must establish, as it were, a new identity. He must increasingly seek independence from adult authority. The peer group assists greatly in helping the child to achieve this new status.

A second developmental task involves the acquisition of attitudes and behavior required of participants in human groups. The new schoolchild must learn how to get along with others and how to share, developing a sense of fairness, a respect for rules, and an understanding of the concept of sportsmanship.

A third required task is that of learning one's appropriate sex role in the society. Parents, adults, and teachers participate in this process by their constant admonitions regarding the ways in which little boys and girls should act. The like-sex peer group plays a significant role in this phase of the socialization process.

Another task to be mastered by the growing child is the development of what often are called conscience and a sense of morality. Although standards and values are acquired primarily from parents, teachers and other significant adults also participate in the process. A number of ideas have been put forward to explain the growth of morality in children, among which are the concepts of identification, modeling, direct tuition, and reinforcement.

The mastery of the fundamental processes of reading, writing, computation, and other related intellectual skills required ultimately for adult participation in life constitute another developmental task of childhood. Also, it is necessary at this age to acquire knowledge, attitudes, and habits related to such key concerns as safety, health, and the care of one's body.

All of these developmental tasks are not equal sources of potential problems in schools and classrooms. A knowledge of the requisite learnings is important, however, if one is seeking to understand the many factors that can operate to make a crucible of many urban classrooms. As the reader will see, problems encountered by children and adolescents in the mastery of developmental tasks can be escalated in severity when they are combined with other ethnic, social and institutional factors.

To become an increasingly independent person requires that the child often contest the decisions and authority of adults. One learns to be independent by gaining experiences at being independent. Parents and teachers are often shocked by the bizarre transitions that can take place in the behavior of children—one minute sweet and obedient in little things, the next moment completely rebellious.

A second problem relates to problems with peers. The preschool child typically enjoys a rather exclusive status in his family. The parental attention to which the child has been conditioned, the special status that he has enjoyed, do not transfer with him to the classes of the kindergarten or primary school. Here he must learn to compete with others for attention, respect, and status. Children who have been treated in overly protected or extremely authoritarian ways at home often find the transition to school extremely difficult. The need for status and recognition from both the teacher and one's peers leads to many kinds of undesirable social behavior, among which are showing-off, selfishness, bullying, verbal and physical attacks on others, and plain disobedience.

Children during the latency period tend to group themselves according to their sex. Such groupings operate to reinforce the social expectations of each particular sex group. These groupings, however, can produce noisy, competitive confrontations; verbal and even physical aggression in some settings; and a constant irritation and concern for the teacher.

When students fail to encounter success in the mastery of

intellectual tasks, they often direct their frustrations against their peers and even the teacher. In inner-city classrooms, this failure is perhaps one of the greatest causes of interpersonal and antisocial behavior problems.

Physical growth, during the elementary school years, differs greatly between the sexes and even among the members of a particular sex group. During the early years, girls tend to mature both physically and socially more quickly than do boys. Discrepancies between the sexes in these two areas can be productive of problems in the classroom. It has been said by some educators that the elementary school in particular discriminates against males because of its emphasis on behaviors that are socially demanded of females. In the earlier grades, girls are the better performers in school from the point of view of grades, and fewer of them present behavior problems in school. Extreme hostility between the sexes in elementary grades can pose severe problems for teachers in some instances.

Physical growth problems or discrepancies are often related to the self-concepts that youngsters have of themselves. If a child's appearance or physical abilities differ markedly from those considered to be ideal and desirable, it is quite possible that he will suffer from feelings of inadequacy and may become the target of the mockery and dislike of his peers.

Some of the developmental tasks mentioned for childhood are repeated at the time of adolescence, but they tend to be more demanding of the preadult. Adolescents in our society are expected to achieve a certain degree of proficiency in certain developmental tasks. They must:

Develop a desirable degree of emotional independence from their parents and other significant adults;

Develop more mature relations with their peers of both sexes;

Learn their socially appropriate sex role as a young adult;

Learn to accept themselves as physical beings regardless of their natural endowments;

Acquire the necessary intellectual concepts and cognitive skills required of self-sufficient citizens in a democratic, technologically oriented society;

Develop a set of appropriate values that direct their behavior;

Decide at least in a general way future vocations or careers.

There is perhaps no more chaotic a period of life as that defined as adolescence. Due to various rapid biopsychological changes that take place at the onset of puberty, the behaviors of early adolescents may reflect great inconsistency. During this period children behave in ways which range from laziness to hyperactivity. Teachers and parents often complain of inattentiveness and daydreaming on the part of adolescents.

The one task that produces great problems both at home and at school involves the adolescent's need for emotional independence from adults and the concurrent need to win the acceptance of his peers. Parents who find it difficult or impossible to allow their adolescents to undergo the process of what might be termed de-satellitization often find themselves in bitter clashes with them. The school and the teacher often get caught in the fallout of such confrontations, with teachers becoming the substitute targets of these parent-offspring conflicts.

Another problem associated with the developmental tasks of adolescence relates to the significance of the peer group. The subculture of this group has great importance for its members in that it is a source of social acceptance, status, prestige, recognition, and independence. As discussed later, the peer group whose values, norms, or standards are at variance with those of the school or adult society can bring about conflicts in the school and with society at large.

Increasingly, youths are displaying problems associated with the task of developing a socially acceptable set of values or an ethical system. Much of this difficulty can be attributed to the inconsistencies that youths see in the lives of adults and in the practices of social institutions which adults command. The mass media also make it difficult to hide these discrepancies between what is preached and what is practiced. More and more, teachers, parents, and other adults find themselves under the searching interrogation of youngsters who question many of the "sacred givens" of the society.

The Family Role in Socialization

The concept of socialization is held to mean the ways in which parents in particular and other significant adults interact with a growing child so as to prepare him for the demands of later life stages. Socialization (or learning) is accomplished through a variety of means. Direct instruction is perhaps the most commonly used practice. Children learn from their parents through the process of imitation or modeling. Further social learning takes place through the application of positive reinforcements or rewards by the socializing agent for proper behavior and negative ones for undesirable behavior. Finally, some psychologists contend that much of socialization involves the process of identification during which the child unconsciously incorporates or accepts as his own the standards and values of his parents.

A child's family gives him far more than just his name. This institution determines to a great extent the social position he will most likely hold in the society, how he will be treated by others, and the opportunities that he will have to improve his status in life. Perhaps its most significant effect is that it helps to shape the picture or image that a child develops of himself.

Thomas S. Langner contends that a person's ego strength or self-image arises primarily from the strength of one's ego-ideal (one's internalized perceptions of his parents and their standards).[10] This view, which is supported by others, implies that from the start the middle-class child is in a position to develop a more positive self-image than is the less fortunate child in the low-income family. David and Pearl Ausubel ascribe this more

favorable situation enjoyed by the middle-class child to the fact
that he enjoys a great deal of status derived simply because of
the status of his parents.[11] Most policemen, for example, would
treat a medical doctor's son (once the fact is known) quite
differently from the way they would the youth known to be from
a broken home in the ghetto section of town, even though both
individuals were arrested for the same offence.

The plight of the low-income parent is a serious one. His
own life status reduces his value as a model to be copied by the
child; he has little to offer in the form of derived status; and
finally, he must often use himself as an example of what the
child should not become in trying to develop motivation in his
offspring.

Before attempting to deal with the possible relations between certain socially desired behavior and parent-child relationships, let us look at several factors which are different in the
process as practiced by the middle- and low-income classes.

According to Urie Bronfenbrenner, an interesting transition in child-rearing practices has taken place since World War
II.[12] Prior to that time, the socialization process as practiced by
middle-class parents was less permissive than that practiced
by low-income parents. The reverse seems to have taken place
since 1945: middle-class parents now surpass low-income parents in permissiveness. His observation is accompanied by the
following statement of concern.

> Our data indicate that the middle-class parents are be-
> coming increasingly permissive in response to the child's
> expressed needs and desires. Yet, those same parents have
> not relaxed their high levels of expectations for ultimate
> performance. Do we have here a typical instance of [Ruth]
> Benedict's "discontinuity in cultural conditioning," with
> the child first being encouraged in one pattern of response
> and then expected to perform in a very different fashion?
> If so, there are days of disappointment ahead for middle-
> class fathers and mothers.[13]

It must be noted that the low-income family experience stresses that its favored counterpart is better able to avoid. As a family unit it has a greater chance of being headed by one parent, who in a greater number of cases is a woman. Its income is considerably lower than that of the middle-class family.

A review of child rearing studies involving the two class groups reveals rather different perceptions regarding parent-child relationships.[14] Middle-class mothers describe their role as that of guiding, understanding, and relating to the child, making sure that the child is happy, shares with others, and is eager to learn. In general these mothers see their role as being an acceptant participant in an egalitarian relationship with their children. Middle-class mothers depicted ideal child behavior by these behavioral indicators: happiness, considerateness, and self-control.

Low-income mothers tend to see their role as a housekeeper first. Regarding their children, their duties are to see that they are kept neat and clean, to train the child to regularity, and to get the child to obey and respect adults. Ideal child behavior for these mothers is described in terms of neatness, cleanliness, and obedience.

Another study of disadvantaged black mothers and middle-class white mothers, by Norma Radin and Constance Kamii, provides additional information regarding the socialization process in these two groups.[15] Low-income mothers are found to believe that infancy is a period of helplessness, and they are eager to wean and toilet train the young. This eagerness may well be a reflection of the pressures under which they live. While wanting their children to be physically independent, the low-income mothers tend to be very protective, intrusive, and controlling. Furthermore, their responses tend to display little respect for the child as an individual. This point should not be misconstrued to be indicative of not loving their children. These black mothers believe in shielding their children from problems.

Such behavior, it should be noted, restricts the child's chances of learning coping behaviors. In general, it seems as though these low-income mothers view the child as having limited potential for developing coping skills and inner control. While the responses of these black mothers indicate that they feel respect for the child is important, and that they believe in sharing his feelings and experiences, yet this group also indicates a strong disinterest in listening to children and their problems (i.e., children should be seen and not heard).

Middle-class white mothers, on the other hand, are found to believe that it is important to expose the child to challenging situations and to support their coping efforts in such situations. These white mothers express a strong belief that parents should respect the privacy of children's thoughts. These parents also evidence a greater willingness to discuss problems brought up by their children.

The Middle-Class Norms of the School

The classroom becomes the arena in which these and other differences in the socialization practices of middle-class and low-income families come into conflict. Whether we want to admit it or not, education in this society has as its basis certain norms that are traditionally associated with the middle class. Not only do these norms govern what the school expects of students, but they also serve as an end in the educative process.

For the purposes of this discussion, the author has selected five of the norms of behavior that are commonly identified as being middle class in character.* An important criterion for the

---

*In his work on delinquent boys, Albert K. Cohen listed some nine behaviors or expectations that he felt were norms of the middle class;[16] earlier Allison Davis and Robert Havighurst had arrived at a similar list of traits.[17] According to Cohen, individuals are expected to: (1) be ambitious, seek success; (2) display individuality and be a responsible and dependable

(footnote continued on next page)

selection of these particular traits was their relevance to the realities of the classroom situation. A particular norm will be stated and followed by a discussion of each of the two social class group's treatment of this particular behavior.

1. *One is not to engage in physical aggression against others.*

Fights and aggressive verbal and physical behavior constitute major problems for the urban teacher. What are some possible explanations for the prevalence of this behavior in certain schools?

Interesting discrepancies exist between the ways in which middle-class and low-income parents react to aggression. Verbal aggression within the family is accorded greater tolerance in the middle-class home.[18] Langner contends that members of this class see the value of verbal combat and seek to develop it in their children. Yet, middle-class parents are less tolerant of verbal aggression against others.

Conversely, Langner reports that low-income parents tend to tolerate less aggression within the family, either verbal or physical.[19] A strong taboo exists in such families against child-to-parent aggression. Low-income parents, however, are more tolerant of verbal and physical aggression against those outside the family when such seems justified.

It is of interest to note that low-income parents tend to use more physical punishment against their children than do middle-class parents.[20] It has been speculated that low-income children tend to be more verbally and physically aggressive against others because they have learned unconsciously from their parents' treatment of them that this is a sanctioned way of punishing others.

---

person; (3) develop socially required skills and display achievement; (4) be willing to delay immediate gratification for later rewards; (5) display rationality at all times; (6) get along with others and do this via proper displays of manners, courtesy, and personality; (7) control tendencies toward physical aggression; (8) engage in constructive use of leisure time; and (9) show respect for property—not take other's property.

2. *One's behavior should always be guided by the use of reason.*

Related to the problem of verbal and physical aggression is the tendency for disadvantaged youngsters to display less control over their impulses. Such a disability leads to frequent confrontations with peers and adult figures. Too often fighting or verbal confrontation are the only means of problem-resolution that disadvantaged learners seem to know. By contrast, as noted earlier, middle-class children are encouraged more by their parents to engage in dialog with them. A boy in such a family who gets into a fight with another lad is more likely to be encouraged to use other ways of handling similar conflicts than would his peer in a low-income family.

Individuals learn to reason and to act rationally only through experiences that have allowed them to develop this form of behavior. Too often the low-income youngster is administered immediate physical punishment without any attempt being made to help him see alternative behavior.

Low-income parents tend to make use of quick, unquestionable disciplinary techniques that are designed to punish the offender for his transgression, whereas middle-class parents are more prone to use what has been called psychological punishment. This form of discipline stresses showing disapproval, isolation of the misbehaving child, the withdrawal of privileges, a reduction in warmth during parent-to-offspring interactions.

3. *One must develop as an individual who is a responsible and dependable person.*

One's perception of himself develops in a large sense out of the responses one receives from others. The extent to which an adult, or a child for that matter, displays a sense of his own identity and acts as a responsible and dependable person must relate to the quality of the image that he has of himself. It is axiomatic in psychology that a person cannot like others unless he also likes himself.

The socialization process of the middle-class home is very effective for training its offspring to develop a sense of identity and individuality. Langner cites several ways in which the middle-class family is able to do this.[21] Because the birthrate in this group is lower than that of the working class, children have less competition for the attention and affection of their parents. Such children do not have to share their toys, clothes, and so forth. It would also appear that the larger the family group the greater the tendency toward impersonality among its members, equanimity being more important than the rights of its individual members. Typically, middle-class families encourage a sense of identity in children through photo albums and baby books (both of which cost money), which help the growing child see the ways in which he changes. Likewise, the middle-class family is accustomed to such rituals as birthday parties that give recognition of the growth and development of the child and reaffirm his acceptance and membership in the family. Langner reports that many poor children never are given the pleasure of birthday parties.

Conversely, a tendency to suppress the development of a sense of identity in children has been found by H. Wortis in a study of low-income black mothers.[22] These mothers displayed a lack of interest in encouraging the personal characteristics of their children that could be used to differentiate one child from another. Such interest on the part of parents is vital if a child is to develop a strong sense of his own identity and worth and to be willing to defend that identity in positive ways.

4. *One must display ambition and seek to be a success in life.*

The middle-class home has been described as having a built-in curriculum that prepares most of its children for school success long before they arrive at its doors. Youngsters from this stratum of society are conditioned early in life to expect to succeed in school, get good grades, and look forward to attending a "good" college or university.[23] Not only are these expectations inculcated into the children of the middle class, but also many of the resources needed to make them come true are provided.

Frances R. Link reports that more middle-class urban and suburban parents continue to live together for the sake of their children.[24] Furthermore, she contends, the children know this and develop feelings of pressure and responsibility for the survival of the marriage and its continued happiness.

In too many cases, children of low-income parents are not aware of what is really required to succeed in school and in certain occupations and professions. They have few illusions about social and economic realities that they face. As observed earlier, low-income parents cannot serve as success models, and children therefore have less reason to look to parents for guidance and inspiration. To paraphrase Ausubel and Ausubel, low-income children and youths, especially black youths, have fewer illusions about parental omniscience for teachers to shatter.[25] The disadvantaged youth is coerced by the norms of his peer group against accepting the authority of the teacher, against seeking her approval, and against entering into a satellite relationship with her.

To this point we have not considered the significance of the peer group. For a variety of reasons, low-income children are watched less closely during the childhood period once they have learned to walk and talk and take care of themselves in general. They enjoy greater freedom to roam their neighborhoods and to engage in unsupervised play. They develop strong ties early with their peer groups, which can border on addiction to its codes and norms. Such a relationship can lead to a precocious sense of independence and greater hostility toward adult authority figures.

5. *One should be willing to delay gratification for the realization of later goals and rewards.*

As Elizabeth Douvan and others have documented, middle-class persons have a greater capacity to delay their need for immediate gratification than do individuals socialized in low-income families.[26] The delayed gratification pattern (DGP) is very important as a requisite for success in a highly literate and technologically advanced society. The person who seeks a college education, for example, is required to postpone such events as entering the labor market, achieving economic independence, and marrying and starting one's family.

The rewards of much of education are realized over a period of time. The person who lives in poverty, who encounters in his personal life few (if any) persons for whom education has paid off, and who sees little hope for any improvement in his situation, is less willing to further complicate his life by daring to dream impossible dreams. The simple demands of existence and survival consume too much of the energy of the poor—energy that could provide the drive for achievement.

A Lower-Class Culture

One way of looking at—and perhaps justifying—most of these norms is to consider them as being essential behavioral traits required of persons living in a complex technological society that seeks to pursue democratic principles. One might offer the hypothesis that the closer a student's socialized behavior approximates the norms, the less difficulty he will encounter with the work and authorities of the school.

On the other hand, in any discussion regarding the education of disadvantaged pupils, the question inevitably arises whether they should be forced to master these middle-class forms of behavior at the expense of their own subcultural norms. Many of these norms are seen by low-income persons as square, straight, or up-tight behaviors. According to Walter B. Miller, there is a growing segment of American society that is developing a way of life, characteristic patterns of behavior, and values constituting a different cultural system, which he terms lower class.

Evidence indicates that this cultural system is becoming increasingly distinctive, and that the size of the group which shares this tradition is increasing. The lower-class way of life, in common with that of all distinctive cultural groups, is characterized by a set of focal concerns—areas or issues which command widespread and persistent attention and a high degree of emotional involvement.[27]

Miller presents six focal concerns that he feels command the energy and attention of what he calls the lower-class culture:

1.	Trouble	law-abiding behavior	law-violating behavior
2.	Toughness	physical prowess, skill, masculinity, daring	timidity, cowardice, caution
3.	Smartness	ability to con, dupe, outsmart, quickness in verbal repartee	gaining money, hard work, slowness, dull-wittedness
4.	Excitement	thrill, risk, danger, activity	boredom, deadness, safeness, sameness, passivity
5.	Fate	favored by fortune, being lucky	ill-omened, being unlucky
6.	Autonomy	freedom from external restraint, freedom from superordinate authority, independence	presence of external constraints, presence of strong authority, dependency, being cared for

Four of these concerns that are particularly relevant to the crucible of the urban classroom are discussed here—toughness, smartness, excitement, and autonomy.

The white student-teacher or new teacher who encounters disadvantaged children or youths (especially blacks) for the first time in a school setting is shocked by the great amount of time and activity devoted to claims and counterclaims of toughness. Many problems result as youngsters seek to validate these claims. Why, then, does this focal concern exist?

To live in a slum and to be poor is, to say the least, a challenging reality; those who can survive psychologically and physically in such circumstances have to be tough. There also are other possible explanations for this concern with toughness and the display of physical aggression. Children who grow up with less adult supervision and have more freedom to move about in their communities learn early the lesson of self-reliance and defense. One learns how to fight and to be aggressive and also how to intimidate the less aggressive and less physically tough peer. It was noted earlier that low-income parents tolerate more extra-family aggression on the part of their children. Such parents may not encourage their children to start fights, but they do expect them to be able to defend themselves if attacked physically. A final explanation is the expectation within the subculture of poverty that men be fearless, brave, and aggressive. In the Latin subcultures this form of expected male behavior is termed *machismo*.

Teachers of the disadvantaged youths are also often plagued by the children's tendency to engage in "smart" behavior. This takes a variety of forms, but the ultimate aim is to embarrass, to humiliate, or to put down another person. Teachers are not immune to being the targets of such behavior. Students who may score low on IQ tests may display the most remarkable verbal ability when engaging in gamesmanship such as capping or signifying (bad-mouthing), in which the objective is to outwit or put down the other person; playing the dozens, or talking in increasingly disparaging terms about each other's mother; and conning behavior, or putting something over on another via a tall tale. Inner-city teachers often complain of the drain on their energies as a result of having to cope with toughness and smart behavior.

To be poor is also often to be bored. Poor families cannot afford experiences that would bring variety into their lives. Some problems encountered in disadvantaged schools are perhaps a reaction to the dullness of a life of poverty, compounded by the dull and unstimulating atmosphere of many classrooms. No doubt because of the sheer frustration born of this boredom, many pupils initiate provoking, disruptive acts to relieve the tension they feel.

Of the four focal concerns under discussion here, autonomy is often the most confusing one to understand and deal with. At one moment low-income persons can be clamoring for independence from others who dominate them and asserting that no one can tell them what to do and at the next moment can display behavior indicating a desire for limitations and strong leadership. These oscillations between the two extremes of autonomy and complete dependency reflect, perhaps, the impact of the unstable, ego-shattering nature of low-income and ethnic minority group status.

The Problems Confronting the Teacher

Central to solving the problems of the urban classroom is the effective preparation of teachers for such settings. While a variety of teacher-education programs seek to produce effective teachers for the inner city, there are no firm guidelines.

Following are selected excerpts from a series of interviews with student teachers assigned to urban classrooms. These comments depict clearly the problems confronting both new and experienced teachers in such situations.

> *Female:* I always complained about unimaginative teachers, and I thought, "Oh my God! Can I be a creative teacher?" I had, when I started, an inferiority complex about my being able to be as good about this as I wanted to be.

> *Female:* I wasn't prepared to teach them—oh, American (literature) stuff. I had all of this eighteenth-century literature that these kids just, you know, it just—nothing! Why

should they have to read this when there are such great books that are being written now that they can relate to and want to come to class for.

Male: Sleeping bugs me because it reflects upon my teaching. If I ask a student whether he has a problem, and he says that he does not and is just bored—it blows my mind!

Female: I felt that every time that I was authoritative, when I was down on them, I'd get these incredible papers (during creative writing). "You ass . . . ." "You white bitch," "You're acting like a ninety-year-old biddy." But they were really, really honest. I'm afraid that many, many times these authoritative teachers don't get to know that because of the way they run their classrooms.

Female: In an inner-city classroom, I have to put my foot down and I don't like it.

Male: When I first started, I felt that I had to be a person who students could approach, could trust, and who could sympathize with them.

Female: I don't know what to do when a student is screaming at me and I can't reason with him. I'm so used to the fact . . . "O.K. let's calm down; let's talk about it." And when the student won't calm down and talk about it—we have quite a few, you know, screaming about race. That is a big thing in my class. "I won't move," "I won't sit down," "Don't touch me," and they just sit there. You hate to have to confront them and say either you do this or leave. They won't respond to you at all. When I can't use reason, I'm lost.

Female: I couldn't see how he (an experienced teacher) could hate the kids when I observed his class. And at the end of the year I could catch myself getting mad at them, thinking nasty things. I said, "Oh! my God," at the beginning of the year—I said, "No person could end up like this."

Female 1: I find that with black kids, I try to be nicer.
Female 2: Oh! That's the white bag.
Female 1: Right! Now I know.

Female: I went in feeling that the teacher had to have respect. This is a part of my background. So, I wanted respect, but I didn't want to be an ogre. I don't know how to get this balance. How was I going to get them to respect me and say, "When she says something, she means it, and yet commands respect and respects you as well." It's a two-sided deal, and then at the same time to be able to break down and be affectionate with students and be concerned with their problems, and yet not make it buddy-buddy. I wanted respect without fear.

Male: I worried about how I could make what I knew into something that they would enjoy and want to learn. I really worried about my ability to conceptualize issues so that my students could relate to them.

The many problems that teachers encounter in urban classrooms help account for the variety of teacher responses. Some of these coping devices or mechanisms further compound the problems already present in the situation. As a means of survival, teachers often strive for the love and affection of the students, many times, unfortunately, at the sacrifice of learning. Other teachers and administrators feel that a very tightly run ship is the best approach. The good student becomes the quiet student, and the good class is a group working noiselessly over its workbooks or ditto-sheets.

Perhaps the greatest tragedy in urban classrooms (or even in suburban ones, for that matter) is to have teachers who sincerely believe that students are incapable of learning and who teach them in this demeaning manner.

It is a well-documented fact that the retention of good, capable, and dedicated teachers in the classrooms of inner-city schools is becoming increasingly difficult. In many instances, 50 per cent of a ghetto area's staff will leave in a given year. More new and less experienced teachers are assigned to such schools, as well as larger numbers of teachers on provisional credentials. Under such circumstances it is difficult, if not impossible, to develop an educational program with continuity, that has a chance of improving the quality of pupil learning.

The crucible of the urban classroom demands a teacher with unusual qualifications. Since most teachers come from family backgrounds quite divergent from those of their inner-city pupils, the proper preprofessional education of these instructors must involve a form of reeducation. Kurt Lewin contends that effective reeducation must affect the personal structures of individuals in order to contribute to real and persistent behavioral changes.[28] He defined such a structure as being bidimensional, comprising the *knowledge* level (cognitive) and *feeling* level (affective). Reeducation has to produce desired changes at both levels.

Thus, teacher education, or education of any kind, must seek to increase the knowledge that a person possesses so that he can restructure it into its most valid and useful forms. An essential body of knowledge for the urban teacher, in addition to knowledge of his subject, must relate to the ethnic groups and subcultures with whom he must deal. He must also be helped to develop the proper attitudes and feelings that make it possible for him to interact effectively with disadvantaged learners and their parents.

Such a reeducation effort cannot be gained from books and lectures alone. Experiences and encounters with the realities of urban life must be a valid part of the preparation experience. Role-playing, creative dramatics, and other affect-producing techniques must be used.

What would seem to be the qualities required of a person who would enter the crucible of the urban classroom and survive its intense emotional, intellectual, and physical demands?

Mario D. Fantini and Gerald Weinstein stress the importance of two qualities which seem essential for teachers in urban schools: strength and sensitivity. Strength is defined as "the ability to initiate an identifiable structure, and to maintain that structure with a certain degree of compellingness and persistence even under exasperating circumstances." Sensitivity is defined as an awareness of the "unique needs of children—from the seeking of cues from the learner, 'reading' or interpreting the cues, seeking more information to clarify cues, and adapting instruction to the cues."[29]

In addition to these qualities, the urban teacher must possess a solid mastery of what he is trying to teach, a sound repertoire of instructional techniques, and a mind that is creative or at least imaginative.

In addition to possessing the above attributes, the effective teacher in the urban classroom must be a person who, above all, loves children. Love is not defined here as outpourings of warmth and good feelings, but rather in the terms used by Erich Fromm to explicate the concept of love in his book, *The Art of Loving*.[30] For Fromm, a person loves another when he makes an effort to *know* the other person as a human being; makes every effort to really *understand* the other person as a unique being; seeks to *respect* the other person for his humanity, regardless of his faults; really *cares* about what is happening to the other person; and is willing to *give of himself* to help the other person who needs such assistance.

If love, as defined above, could become the central, guiding force in all of our lives, a paper with this topic and emphasis would not be needed.

The Dogmas of Pedagogy

A major factor that contributes to problems of the urban classroom is the often nebulous nature of the goals and purposes of both the school and its teachers. Look at the statement of philosophy or the course of study of almost any school district: you will be hard pressed to find just what students are expected to learn, be able to do, and at what levels of competency they are expected to perform. More than ever, schools and their teachers need to consider carefully just what they expect their pupils to learn and to devise means of getting the most objective information possible about the achievement of these goals.

What has been and still is lacking in education are (1) a clear-cut, objective specification of just what the school and its teachers are (or should be) trying to do; and (2) some system of accountability that assesses the extent to which these goals or ends are being realized.

In too many cases, school systems, administrators, and teachers lack either the willingness, ability, or courage to break the bounds of traditional approaches to the education of youngsters with whom they have failed. Urban schools and classrooms that seek to educate disadvantaged students quite obviously should be the most flexible, creative, and vitally alive settings possible. Yet one has but to look at experimental or innovative programs for inner-city schools to see that these efforts, as well as traditional compensatory education ventures, still respect such sacred concepts as the class period and equal time for various subjects.

There is an appalling gap in pedagogy between avowed belief and actual practice. From his observations of what educators and teachers *really* do, Carl Rogers identifies six assumptions that he feels principally guide their behavior.[31]

The student cannot be trusted to pursue his own learning. Educators "look suspiciously on the student's aims and desires and devote their energies to guiding him along the pathway he *should* follow."

Presentation equals learning. Educators contend that the lesson plan or the curriculum defines what is learned. Rogers contends that this approach fails to tap the actual experiences of the students during a particular "learning" experience.

The aim of education is to accumulate brick upon brick of formal knowledge. This view assumes that there must be a foundation of knowledge and, further, that once learned something is never forgotten.

The truth is known. Textbooks and knowledge are presented as the ultimate ends of a quest. Students are not encouraged to see that the search for knowledge and its refinement and modification are never-ending.

Constructive and creative citizens develop from passive learners.

Evaluation is education, and education is evaluation.

Rogers' criticisms are directed at education in general. They are, nonetheless, applicable in the case of the education of disadvantaged learners. He feels that education can be improved only if the incorporation of the *processes* of learning and changing become its deepest purposes.

Nathaniel Hickerson's primary concern in recent studies has been the isolation of factors in American public education that are contributing to alienation in students. His basic criticism centers upon six propositions that he contends provide a basic structure for our educational practices.[32]

1. *Native* intelligence is measurable.

2. Our devices used for measuring children's intelligence are sufficiently accurate to be relied upon.

3. Only certain children are capable of academic education in depth.

4. Children capable of academic education in depth can be identified, in the majority of cases, in the early years of elementary education.

5. Program tracks other than the academic should be provided for children incapable of academic school work.

6. The school must help the student to adjust realistically to his abilities and potentialities as determined primarily by intelligence and achievement-measuring tests and devices.

Hickerson's criticisms are quite relevant to the problems faced by disadvantaged learners. Such pupils often enter "verbally dominated" schools with a form of nonstandard English, with smaller standard English vocabularies, and with less readiness for the task of reading. Is there any wonder that children who start the race through the schools from so handicapped a position grow to resent school and teachers and to engage in escapist behavior? Another point inherent in Hickerson's list is a criticism of the tracking system, which in too many instances literally determines a student's educational future from the beginning. What does it do to a student's perception of himself when he learns that powers over which he has little or no control have designated him as a C-track student, with C-track ability and almost definitely a class C future?

The concept of the IQ as a valid measure of all of the intellectual capacities and potentials of human beings is one of the most dehumanizing ideas that still is sacred in some halls of the educational establishment. These devices have doomed innumerable disadvantaged students to levels of educational attainment and to occupations far beneath their potentials.

The crucible of the urban classroom can be made less severe only if educators are willing to become heretics to the dogma of the IQ test. This static view of a statistical ratio as being a valid measure of a person's potentialities has shackled education for over fifty years. Education needs to develop a view of human potential and ability which is dynamic and capable of continuous growth. If schools dared to take this course, much of the tracking and grouping that creates so many problems for disadvantaged students in particular would have to be abandoned. Human performance and growth would then become the real indicators of human potential. One can expect only bitter hostility from a class that has been placed in a C section and told that, regardless of how hard they work or how much they learn, their highest grade can only be a C.

The Reform of the Curriculum

The curriculum of the schools has come under much fire recently for being out of date and for lacking relevance and validity. Perhaps the best statement regarding the curriculum of the disadvantaged school (or others for that matter) has been offered by Fantini and Weinstein in a 1967 monograph.[33] They contend that much of contemporary curriculum fails to be effective because it does not really make contact with the lives of learners. They suggest two general criteria for curriculum: it should be functional, starting "where the child is" in his development, and it must be developmental in that the immediate world or stage of development of the child is extended and interrelated with greater portions of the world around him.

Specifically they suggest eight changes that the curriculum must make if it is to be relevant and effective. The curriculum in the schools must change:

1. From a curriculum that is prepackaged and uniform to one that is flexible and geared to the needs of students in individual schools in the system.

2. From a curriculum that is symbol-based (pictures and words) to one that is experience-based.

3. From a horizontally programmed, disjointed sequence of skills to a vertically programmed, small-step sequence of skills where the learner can see where he is and where he has to go.

4. From curriculum that is past- and future-oriented to one that is immediate-oriented.

5. From a *what* curriculum (e.g., What is poverty?) to a *why* curriculum (e.g., Why is poverty allowed to exist?).

6. From a completely academic curriculum which stresses *knowing* or memorizing knowledge to one geared to social participation which stresses *doing* and being involved with things in one's own life.

7. From an antiseptic curriculum to one that attempts to explore reality (e.g., Who really owns the ghetto?).*

8. From emphasis solely on cognitive, extrinsic content to equal emphasis on affective, inner content (e.g., learner's feelings and concerns).

In offering the idea of the contact curriculum, Fantini and Weinstein contend that the curriculum that "makes the most contact is that which is most relevant to them (disadvantaged students) and which makes a connection between the affective or feeling aspects and the cognitive or conceptualizing aspects of the learner."

---

*Fantini and Weinstein define an "antiseptic" curriculum as one that ignores totally the interests and problems of the student, and the reality of their living. Of course, not all educators try to avoid dealing with these realities. But mistakes can be made when attempts at relevance are ill-conceived or when they take place without adequate interpretation. An example of this is cited by these authors in which a ghetto schoolteacher tried to have her students discuss questions regarding life in slums, integration, and discrimination. The youngsters are reported to have entered the discussion for a while as if talking about situations and people removed from them. After a while, resentment and anger began to take over, and the pupils complained about having to talk about such things. They wanted, they said, to study their regular subjects. Such misguided efforts fall into a subcategory that the authors term the "semiantiseptic" curriculum.[34]

Another dimension of the curriculum issue should be emphasized here. There is a crying need to make the content of the curriculum both valid and accurate as to the past history and present status of the ethnic minorities in this country. This need is particularly true in the case of blacks, Mexican-Americans, and American Indians.*

A final positive step that the school might undertake involves developing new formats for instruction. The idea of all students in a single class studying the same material at the same time is a travesty upon the idea of the individualized nature of learning. Individualized instruction, tuition, team learning, and ungraded structures, among many other possible innovations, need to be explored.

A New Climate in the Schools

As observed earlier, schools do not exist in a vacuum. What takes place in the total social environment greatly affects what takes place in schools and in classrooms. Educators in urban settings may develop more relevant curricula. They may develop the most effective instructional techniques possible. But if students look about them and see a society that is marked by a lack of equal opportunity for all citizens—a society that seems unconcerned about the needs of large segments of the population, which is racist in feelings, attitudes, and behavior, and which seems hardly concerned about the quality of human life— just how much of a commitment to learning and to this society will students make?

The problems of the teacher in the urban classroom will be made easier when the social climate in which he works reinforces what he is saying to students; when students can see the real possibility of acceptance and equal opportunity in their

*For a full discussion of this point, see Chapter 5, "Relevance and Self-Image in the Urban School."

lives regardless of their ethnic or class origins; and when they can see a society truly dedicated to the value and dignity of human life. Unless society at large is willing to seek these ends, it has little right to expect educators to be very much more effective than they are at present.

Until racism or, rather, antihumanism is eradicated from American life, large numbers of our children and youth cannot believe in the society. Why should students who know that they would not be fully accepted by the dominant and advantaged segment of the society accept its knowledge, values, and precepts?

One main key to increasing the supportive role of the low-income family in the socialization and educational process is dependent upon the extent to which the scourge of poverty can be removed from their backs. Poor families are too often large families; they are families under stress; they are often incomplete families in the sense that both parents may not be present in the home. Such institutions cannot prepare their youngsters properly with the "hidden" curriculum that is present in the middle-class home. In most cases, poor parents are unaware of both what the school expects of their children as well as of the specific goals that educators claim to have.

Furthermore, the poor parents whose children attend many urban classrooms need to be educated as to how they can become positive, supportive factors in the education of their children. The development of such a program of learning must be initiated by the personnel of the school. Unless educators in disadvantaged areas are willing to undertake this form of leadership, they have little right to accuse the parents of disadvantaged students of disinterest and apathy.

Ways must be found to involve actively these parents in the workings of the school. The "new careers" approach, which makes use of parents in a variety of ways in the school, should be expanded. Not only does this form of parental involvement enhance the possibility of more effective school-community communication, but it also provides an opportunity for these parents to become aware of the importance of their roles in the educational process and to improve their own educational attainment.

Another means for increasing parental involvement in schools, despite the lack of widespread acceptance at present or in the near future, is still worthy of consideration now, even if only on an experimental basis. Parents in poor areas should be given the opportunity to control the financial resources and to make necessary policy decisions regarding the schools in their communities. As of now, the poor have only limited ways of trying to bring about needed educational change in their areas, and the only effective tactic seems to be confrontation and disruption. Once people have the control of an institution, they also inherit the responsibility for insuring its continued success. One does not generally learn responsibility without opportunities to practice being responsible.

The strongest allies of the urban school and teacher are the parents of the students in such schools. Too often the school and its staff make no effort to involve these important adults in meaningful ways. A fear of parental interference in the affairs of the school pervades much of urban education. A school in a disadvantaged area should not fail to make use of so valuable a source of assistance.

If the school—whether in suburbia or the inner city—is going to be an effective institution for the development of democratic citizenship, it must be a democratic institution itself. Its staff, at all levels, must reflect the multi-ethnic nature of American society; in addition, staff assignments must reflect a policy of equal opportunity based on ability. With a dearth of success models available to students in disadvantaged areas, it becomes more imperative that the school take up the slack in this respect.

Another essential task of the school is to create an environment which truly reflects respect for the dignity and worth of all of its participants, be they red, yellow, black, or white; young or old; rich or poor. Democratic attitudes, values, and humanistic behavior cannot be learned in a context from which they are absent.

Although the shifting populations of the inner city make desegration more difficult, it is essential that the school, whenever and wherever possible, be a desegregated institution. Ignorance of other races and social class groups can be productive of both fear and hate. Where groups in the society oppose the desegregation of education, it becomes the duty of educators to lead the fight for the realization of this goal, which is so crucial to the vitality and growth of a democratic society.

4. Increasing Educational Opportunity: Research Problems and Results

James S. Coleman

Since the early 1960's, attention in education has moved increasingly toward the educationally disadvantaged. The phrase "equality of educational opportunity" has become more and more common in America and has spread into Europe.*

The Civil Rights Act of 1964 contained an expression of this concern in directing the Commissioner of Education to carry out a survey of the "lack of equality of educational opportunity" by race and other social criteria. The resulting survey, published in July 1966 under the title *Equality of Educational Opportunity*, sometimes known as the Coleman report, constituted one step in the development of knowledge about the extent and causes of educational disadvantage.[1] In the present paper, I will take that report as a starting point, first reviewing its results and then examining the subsequent activities, both in research and in social policy, that have occurred in the five years since its publication.

The survey of equality of educational opportunity came at a time when the very concept of equality of educational

---

*For example, the Organization for Economic Cooperation and Development (OECD) has initiated a program on equality of educational opportunity in the Center for Educational Research and Innovation.

opportunity was in flux. Educators had traditionally measured the quality of a school by various measures of inputs to the school: per pupil expenditure, degrees held by teachers, laboratory facilities, number of books in the school library, and other similar factors. And a large portion of the discussion about inequality of educational opportunity was a discussion of inequality in these input variables. At the same time, substantive questions about effects of schools were being asked rather widely. What were the causes of educational disadvantage for black children and children of other minorities? What was the contribution of school and of home to the low levels of achievement these children exhibited? Did schools reduce or increase the relative disadvantage with which some children began school?

Consequently, a somewhat different conception of equality of educational opportunity was developing from the traditional one based on "school quality," that is, on the input characteristics of schools. The newer conception is based on the actual results of schooling, i.e., the achievement of students. In this view, equality of educational opportunity exists when the *outputs* of schools are equal, not when the inputs of schools are equal.

This conception, however, creates more problems than it solves. Does equality of opportunity (by race, for example) exist according to this definition when black and white children from *equal* family backgrounds achieve equally, or only when black and white children from *unequal* family backgrounds achieve equally? Obviously, if it is the former, this means that the inequalities of family background are merely preserved by the school. If it is the latter, a demand is being imposed on the school to compensate for all the out-of-school differences that lead to differences in academic performance.

Despite this conceptual problem, the shift from a focus on inputs to outputs of educational institutions was under way when the survey was undertaken in 1965. Consequently, the survey examined inequalities in both inputs and outputs and attempted to answer some of the questions about effects of school inputs on educational output. I will not discuss the survey in detail but will briefly review the results in three areas.

Inputs. The first surprising result of the survey was that there was far less inequality of educational inputs among the advantaged and disadvantaged than was commonly supposed. A general misconception existed that there were very wide discrepancies between the expenditures and facilities of schools attended by lower-class blacks and those attended by middle-class whites. The report showed that this was not so; although there were strong regional variations in school inputs and some urban-rural variations, the variations by race within metropolitan areas were not large and were sometimes in favor of black children. This reflects in part the fact that schools in central cities often cost more to run and maintain than those in the suburbs in order to carry out the same activities.

The largest difference in school inputs when variations by race, region, and urban-rural location were examined was between the Southeast and the rest of the country. The second largest was between urban and rural schools in all regions, with schools in urban areas showing somewhat greater inputs. Racial differences were smaller than either of these. Among different school inputs, the greatest variation by race was not an aspect of physical facilities or curricula but of the teachers of blacks and whites. This was particularly pronounced in the South, where the racial matching of teacher and student was still prevalent. Teachers of blacks and whites differed less in respect to formal criteria, such as degrees and experience, than in actual skills and attitudes.

If one considers the characteristics of other students to be inputs of the school, then obviously the racial segregation of American schools causes these to be the greatest differences in school inputs experienced by the average black and the average white. The classmates of the average white and the average black differed, of course, in racial composition; but they differed as well in family educational background, in school achievement, in attitude toward school, and in plans for further education.

Outputs. The survey measured achievement in verbal and mathematical skills in the first, third, sixth, ninth, and twelfth grades, and in certain other skills at grades nine and twelve. It found major differences between whites and Orientals on the one hand, and blacks, Puerto Ricans, Mexican-Americans, and American Indians on the other. Blacks, for example, were about one standard deviation below whites in the first and third grades. (One standard deviation difference means that about 15 per cent of blacks are above the white average and about 15 per cent of whites below the black average.) At higher grades, the difference remains the same in the urban North, but blacks in the South fall progressively below whites, farthest below in the rural South. The end result is that blacks in the rural South are about two standard deviations below whites in the urban North at the twelfth grade, meaning that only about 2.5 per cent of them are above the average of whites in the North.

Comparing blacks regionally and by rural-urban location, the result is as follows: they are at about the same point in the first grade but they diverge, with those in the urban North ending highest and those in the rural South ending lowest. Thus, despite the fact that the urban experience is a bad one for many blacks and the fact that school in urban black ghettos is often an equally bad experience, achievement of urban blacks is better in later grades of school than that of their rural counterparts. The graph on the following page shows some of these achievement differences at different grade levels and in different settings.

Effects of inputs on outputs. Some of the most important questions asked about educational disadvantage concern not merely the degree of inequality of opportunity but the factors that bring it about or ameliorate it. One major question concerns the relative influence of home and school, another concerns the relative influence of various factors within the school. The survey examined the second of these questions, and some evidence was obtained on the first question as well in the course of the analysis.

**Patterns of Achievement in Verbal Skills
at Various Grade Levels by Race and Region**

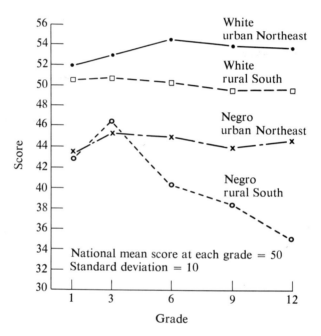

Source: James S. Coleman, "Equality of Educational Opportunity, Reexamined," *Socio Economic Planning Sciences,* Vol. 2 (April 1969) numbers 2, 3, 4, Pergamon Press. Reprinted with permission.

For convenience, the school factors experienced by a given student can be grouped into three classes: school facilities and curricula, characteristics of teachers, and characteristics of other students. Results of the analysis showed that variations in the first of these clusters accounted for negligible variations in achievement; that variations in the second accounted for somewhat more, with teachers' verbal skills constituting the most important characteristic among those measured; and, finally, that variations in the third cluster of factors (characteristics of other students) accounted for the largest amount of variation in achievement.

The implications of these results were principally (1) that the efficiency of those school factors ordinarily considered to be aspects of school "quality" are very low and that the school, as a productive system, does not appear to be very efficient; and (2) that the policy with most promise for increasing achievement of the disadvantaged is integration with children from more advantaged backgrounds, whereby a change can be effected in the one school input that shows the strongest relation to achievement.

Evidence was also obtained on the relative importance of the child's own family background and the school for his academic performance. The survey found that the child's background accounted for considerably more variation in achievement than did the school; taken together, all the school factors together were found to be considerably less important for his achievement than certain aspects of his background, such as his parents' educational level. I should caution that this result could not be directly inferred from the report's analysis because the analysis was not designed to compare the importance of family and school; the analysis, however, strongly suggests this conclusion. (Subsequent analyses of the data directed to this question have confirmed this inference.)

Nearly all these results of the survey were disputed, and a number of analysts took one or another of the results as a challenge. The research generated in this fashion, together with that which stemmed from other sources but addressed itself to education of the disadvantaged, has modified these conclusions in various ways and has led to a number of additional conclusions. We will now turn to some of this research under several headings, first examining that research which was directly derivative from or related to the report.

Research Derivative from the Report

Perhaps the most important result of the report on *Equality of Educational Opportunity* was not the questions it answered but those it asked. By focusing its attention on the outputs of education and the effects of schools on these outputs, the report accelerated the existing shift from inputs to outputs, thus helping to change the discourse about education of the disadvantaged from the characteristics of schools they attend to their effectiveness. Thus, most of the research directly derivative from the report is research on this question. Much of the research consisted of further analysis of the data gathered in the survey, with the aim either of refuting the results of the report or of extending them.

The Harvard seminar. In the 1966–67 academic year, a faculty seminar on the report was organized by Daniel P. Moynihan and Thomas F. Pettigrew at Harvard University. This seminar initiated the reanalysis of several aspects of the survey, carried out by Moynihan, Marshall Smith, Christopher Jencks, and others.[2] The reanalyses largely confirm the qualitative conclusions described above without arriving at any major new ones (an exception is a paper by John F. Kain and Eric A. Hanushek, discussed later in the chapter). Some mistakes in the original analysis were found, but these did not alter the above conclusions. An explicit comparison of the effects of home and school was carried out, and the results showed what the earlier analysis had suggested: that variations in schools account for much less variation in achievement than do variations in home background. Altogether, this is the most extensive set of reanalyses of the report's data, and they largely confirm (and in some places refine) the conclusions.

Analysis of racial isolation in the schools. Almost immediately following the publication of *Equality of Educational Opportunity*, the Civil Rights Commission initiated analysis which led to publication of a 1967 report entitled *Racial Isolation in the Public Schools*.[3] This report contained an extension of the analysis of the survey data by James M. McPartland, designed to examine these questions: When other factors are controlled, is it the social composition of the school as a whole or of the classroom that is related to performance? What is the effect on performance of the disadvantaged of length of time in an integrated school setting: What is the effect on performance of varying racial composition of a school from zero to 100 per cent? Is the "integration effect" an effect of racial integration or of social-class integration?[4]

McPartland extended the analyses of these questions in a doctoral dissertation as well. His findings are:

First, that it is the social composition of the classroom rather than that of the school which is associated with differences in achievement.

Second, that the effects of integration appear roughly to be linearly cumulative over the years in school.

Third, that effects of integration are not linear over school racial or social class composition, but that performance of both black and white students is uniformly higher in schools where about 50 per cent or more of the students are white and uniformly lower in schools where a majority are black.

Fourth, that the effects of integration are largely due to social class or educational background, but that when social class is controlled there remains a small increment in performance of both blacks and whites where the majority of students are white.

This same report included an analysis of data from a single city, Richmond, California, which had been intensively studied by Alan Wilson, examining much the same questions as the original report. Wilson was not able to examine effects of school characteristics but did find an effect on achievement due to social class composition (not racial composition) of the school, much as in the report.

Critiques by economists. The report was subjected to extensive critiques by three pairs of economists: Samuel Bowles and Henry M. Levin; Glen G. Cain and Harold W. Watts; and Eric A. Hanushek and John F. Kain whose study has been previously mentioned.[5] These critiques were directed at a number of aspects of the report but focused principally on the form of the analysis. The reanalysis by Hanushek and Kain produced the principal substantive result to emerge from these studies. It showed that if school facilities and teacher characteristics are grouped together, then, under certain special conditions, the effect of the combined cluster is greater than that of the "other students." Hanushek and Kain do not argue, however, that the effect of school factors, thus redefined, is greater than that of student-body factors. They merely aim to reopen the question and are more interested in methodological questions than substantive ones.

In general, these critiques and reanalysis were motivated by an emerging interest on the part of economists in finding a production function for schools, while the report's results gave no encouragement for any simple production function. The major methodological criticisms concern the use of a measure other than multiple regression coefficients to compare the relative effects of different factors, and the use of a linear regression model rather than one in the form of a Cobb-Douglas production function.* Both these critiques have some validity, and there are reasonable arguments for both the approach used in the report and that argued by the economists. In any case, the substantive conclusions of the report appear little affected by these changes.

Reanalysis by the U.S. Office of Education. As the result of further analyses of the survey data for *Equality of Educational*

---

*Product $= ax_1{}^{b_1}x_2{}^{b_2} \ldots x_n{}^{b_n}$, where x_i are input factors.

Opportunity, carried out under the direction of George W. Mayeske at the U.S. Office of Education, a report titled *Our Nation's Schools* was published in 1969.[6] This report uncovered one important fact related to the questions at hand. While reconfirming the earlier finding that going to one school or another appears to have relatively small effects on achievement, the Mayeske study shows this factor has greater effects on attitudes toward education and aspirations toward further education. Thus, by taking academic achievement as the only output of school, the report overlooked the much stronger effects of school characteristics on other elements that are also outputs of education.

Conference on teacher effects. Early in 1970, Alexander Mood, under whose general direction the survey leading to the original report on the *Equality of Educational Opportunity* had been carried out, chaired a conference on effects of teachers convened by the Office of Education. Most of the papers in this conference contained reanalyses of the data from the report, but some were of newly gathered data. The results of both of the report data and the new data were quite consistent. Teachers' characteristics showed a stronger relation to the child's performance than any other school factors (not including characteristics of other students) and the one characteristic of teachers most strongly and consistently related to the child's performance was the teacher's verbal skill.

Compensatory Programs and Integration

In the past several years, a number of localities have instituted programs involving racial integration or special compensatory programs for the disadvantaged. Some of these programs, which have now been in effect long enough for evaluation, have special virtues for the purposes of comparative research. For example, in some cities where school integration has taken place, a fraction of the black students, randomly selected, is moved from all-black schools to predominantly white schools. Similarly, in some compensatory education programs, schools in which programs take place can be compared to those in which there is no special program.

Recently, a broad survey of the results of these local programs has been undertaken by the New York State Department of Education. The resulting comprehensive report, entitled *Racial and Social Class Isolation in the Schools,* by Robert P. O'Reilly, reviews compensatory and integration programs throughout the United States.[7] The compensatory programs reviewed are generally "enrichment" programs, which reduce the pupil-teacher ratio, usually provide new curricula, and sometimes involve special training of teachers.

The most extensive, one of the most expensive, and the most controversial compensatory program is the More Effective Schools program in New York City, which has been copied in several other cities. Begun as a project organized by the Teacher's Union, the MES program doubled the per pupil expenditure and halved the class size. Careful achievement testing was carried out, but evaluation of the results led to a continuing dispute. The outside evaluation, carried out by the Center for Urban Education, found no effects of the program on achievement, while the program's sponsors within the New York City school system found beneficial effects from the same data.[8] From an examination of the data as presented in the two reports, my conclusion is that there are temporary increments in achievement but that scores revert back to expected levels after the first year. The results appear real (that is, not merely due to chance) but temporary. There does, however, appear to be a continuing increment in positive attitudes toward the school and a general increase in teacher morale.

The results of many compensatory programs appear to parallel those of MES. The achievement is either the same as that of students without the program, or there is a temporary increment that vanishes after the first year.

After reviewing various programs, O'Reilly arrives at a summary that distinguishes three different types of changes: racial integration, compensatory programs, and compensatory programs with racial integration. He finds that (1) compensatory programs alone show little if any effect on achievement; (2) racial integration alone shows some positive effects on achievement of blacks, no effects on that of whites; and (3) the combination of the two shows a greater effect on black achievement than does racial integration alone.

It should be said, however, that though there are points of consistency, some of the results differ from one city to another. For example, planned integration was instituted in Ann Arbor, Michigan, and in three New York cities, Buffalo, Rochester, and White Plains. In none of the four cities was achievement of whites affected, positively or negatively, and in all four the interracial attitudes of both whites and blacks improved. However, in White Plains and Ann Arbor there was no effect of integration on achievement of blacks, while in Buffalo and Rochester there was a substantial positive effect. Generally, there appear to be frequent cases of both types of results in programs of planned school integration: increased achievement of black students or unchanged achievement relative to that expected in all-black schools.

Altogether, the results of local programs suggest that compensatory programs in the ghetto with no racial integration are generally not effective for achievement, though they do lead to more positive attitudes; integration with no compensatory programs shows small increments in achievement; and integration with a compensatory program shows a considerable increment in achievement. O'Reilly's policy inference is that the effectiveness of combining the programs is sufficiently greater not to warrant the use of either program alone.

One of the largest enrichment or compensatory programs is Head Start, a program for four- and five-year-olds both in the summer and during the school year. Head Start is a combined health-and-education program, with an attempt to involve mothers in the program and to utilize indigenous community resources as much as possible. Head Start began with high expectations concerning the impact on school performance of increasing the child's readiness—his familiarity with letters and numbers. The several evaluations of Head Start, most prominently a controversial evaluation by Westinghouse Learning Corporation, yield essentially the same result noted in the case of other compensatory programs.[9] Head Start shows no permanent academic effects. There is a temporary increment beyond what would otherwise be expected of children from comparable backgrounds ordinarily at the beginning of the first year following the Head Start experience, but it is gone by the end of the year. The result is similar to a number of other compensatory programs.

The Timing of Intervention

Several recent studies emphasize the significant policy implications that are involved in the timing of intervention. Benjamin S. Bloom argues in his book *Stability and Change in Human Characteristics* that learning capabilities are established at a very early age and are relatively immutable after this early age.[10] Bloom's inferences are based on the predictability of later IQ and achievement test scores from earlier IQ and achievement test scores. These results show the very high predictability of later scores from earlier ones and thus the very high stability of mental aptitudes after an early age.

Such findings would imply the need for very early intervention, since relative stability is reached by school age and any intervention after that time runs into the fixity of mental skills that is shown by Bloom's work. If this fixing is as certain as Bloom's work implies, it offers a rather gloomy outlook for any attempts in later elementary or secondary school to overcome educational deprivation.

However, the inference is not quite as strong as this because of the nature of Bloom's data, which is not based on instances of special intervention. Thus, what may appear to be the early fixing of mental skills may be due merely to the fact that the child's environment continues unchanged. According to this argument, the mental skills a child will have at nine years of age can be predicted with fair accuracy on the basis of his mental skills at the age of six, not because these were fixed at six, rather because the environment for that child will be about the same during these three years. Even where there have been interventions or changes in the environment, these have often been relatively minor, and the question remains how stable these mental skills would be if there were radical changes in the environment.

Consequently, the optimum age for interventions in the child's environment remain an open question. A number of investigators have become convinced that very early intervention is required if long-term changes in the child's mental skills are to take place. But this position does not have, I believe, sufficiently strong evidence in its favor to justify concentrating on early childhood learning. (It may be desirable to develop early childhood centers to enable mothers to work or for other reasons, but this is a separate question.) There is also the phenomenon, frequently observed, of young people or adults learning to read after having been resistant throughout school— apparently as a consequence of seeing for the first time its necessity for adult activities.

The Effects of the Environment

There are some other results concerning the timing of interventions and the timing of achievement changes that give some additional hints concerning the way in which environmental factors affect learning. A persistent finding is that an intervention (such as Head Start or a compensatory program) leads to an increase in the growth rate of achievement; then the intervention is removed, and the achievement level reverts to what would have been expected.

Still another research project shows the same general pattern. In New York City schools, tests were given at the beginning and end of the school year, from the second through the eighth grade. By linking these tests together, it is possible to approximate the academic progress of the average student from the second through the eighth grades.

The schools were grouped into classes by racial composition, and tests were averaged by school. At the two extremes, the test scores linked in this fashion gave estimates of the progress of the average white student (in all-white schools) and the average black student (in all-black schools). When these "growth" curves were compared, it was found that the slopes *during* the school year were much more similar for blacks and whites than the slopes between school years over the summer months. During these summer periods, the black averages grew only very slightly or in some cases actually declined, while the white averages continued to climb at a rate only a little less than during the school year.*

These results must be confirmed by further studies that compare the differential rates of intellectual growth of children in middle-class and slum environments when the school's influence is removed. However, the findings thus far would seem to indicate that the effect of the environment is not merely to give children different starting points; it persists as a continuing force that can reduce the school's influence.

This recurring pattern (i.e., temporary gains when some special program is initiated and relapses when the program is

---

*This research has some methodological problems, the most serious of which is possible bias introduced by teachers in black schools helping their students in the spring tests to make their own performance appear better. The findings, therefore, must be confirmed by further research before strong inferences are drawn from it.

stopped) suggests some very definite points about the kind of effect the ambient environment has on a child's learning. Three hypotheses seem reasonable a priori:

1. *The environment primarily has an effect in determining the amount of cognitive skill with which a child begins education.* If this is the primary effect of environment, then increasing a child's level of skill at one time should move him to a higher learning curve, resulting not merely in an upward displacement of the learning curve but in increased rates of growth from that time on. This is the implicit hypothesis behind Head Start.

2. *The environment primarily has an effect on the rate of growth.* Thus, when the environment is changed by a special program, the growth rate is increased; when the special program stops, the growth rate reverts to that characteristic of the preexisting environment. If this is the primary effect, the special program should give an upward displacement of the growth curve, but the rate of growth (i.e., of learning) in subsequent periods should be unaffected.

3. *The environment primarily has an effect on the level of academic skill attained.* The environment's effect is to hold or pull the level of attainment toward a level that is compatible with the environment. If this is the primary effect, then a special program should show a temporary increase in rate of growth; but when this special program is stopped, the *level* of attainment will revert to that compatible with the old environment, even if the rate of growth thereby becomes negative for a period.

The various results from special programs are most consistent with the third hypothesis: that the primary effect of the environment is to hold the attainment level of the person in it to a level compatible with that of the environment.* This means,

---

*There is some research on adult *un*learning which confirms this. In tests carried out some period of time after formal education is finished, it is found that adults forget, or unlearn, those skills which they do not use in their day-to-day activities, but they remember and even continue to learn those which they use regularly.

if it is true, that the effects of special temporary programs will not only fail to have a multiplier effect (as implied by the first hypothesis) but will even fail to provide a lasting increment (as implied by the second) and are thus a complete waste of resources. However, a change that is long in time and geographically concentrated so as to change the environmental activities themselves should have a lasting effect, possibly even a multiplier effect. Perhaps even more to the point, it is possible to change the environmental demands on a child outside school through certain kinds of work programs or other activities. The research results imply that if such changes in activities require higher levels of literacy and other intellectual skills, the learning will take place to bring the skills to a level compatible with the environment—even without any special attempts to bring about learning through teaching. In other words, it may be possible to have a greater impact on the development of mental skills by modifying the environmental activities of disadvantaged children, so as to require the use of those skills, than by modifying the "learning environment" in the school while maintaining the same external environment.

Obviously, the implications of these research results are important enough to warrant further research to confirm or disconfirm the hypothesis. This is one of those rare circumstances in social science when a critical experiment is possible. Each of the three hypotheses stated above about the processes through which environmental effects take place is tenable at present, and at least the first two have been implicitly held as assumptions behind certain policy interventions. A critical experiment, with rather simple design, can distinguish between them and thus have enormous impact on the directions of educational changes.

To sum up, it is clear that in a broad and rather cursory review such as this, that the questions necessary for enlightened policy have been only raised and not conclusively answered. It should be recognized, however, that policy decisions are being made every day and do not wait on definitive research conclusions. For example, the many programs of short-term intervention such as Head Start did not wait on definitive conclusions concerning the kind of impact the ambient environment has subsequent to an intervention period. Perhaps more important, a number of policy decisions involving school desegregation have been made based on the conclusions from the report on the *Equality of Educational Opportunity* that the socioeconomic composition of a child's school is an important factor in his achievement. This has occurred largely through (1) local school boards that have initiated a policy of planned school integration and (2) the courts. Several recent court decisions in large cities have argued that because of the effects of school segregation on achievement, school segregation, however arrived at, constitutes a denial of equal educational opportunity and thus is a violation of the Fourteenth Amendment.

While further research has on the whole confirmed the conclusion that segregation reduces achievement of lower-class blacks, it cannot by any means be regarded as absolutely confirmed.

The inexorable need for society to make decisions — that is, to set new policies in education — underscores the necessity for resolving some of the most crucial questions quickly. Some of these questions, and some indications of the answers toward which present research results point, have been described above.

5. Relevance and Self-Image in the Urban School

Larry L. Leslie
and
Ronald C. Bigelow

In the broad and intense controversy over our urban schools, few issues arouse greater emotion among both the white majority and the ethnic minorities than those relating to the curriculum. Vocal leaders are demanding language courses in the original mother tongue of one or another of the minority groups, special emphasis on minority-group history and literature, and the introduction of various instructional techniques and materials designed to preserve or even to resurrect minority cultures. Their byword is "relevance" as the teaching of Chaucer, the Hundred Years' War, and dangling participles is questioned. Although curriculum decision makers generally recognize the validity of various of these and similar charges, the process of change has indeed been slow.

Members of the educational establishment view these developments with alarm. They see them as intrusions by laymen into the domain of the professional. Educators are victims of the most pervasive affliction of American education: its entrapment in history and tradition. *A Tale of Two Cities* has always been taught to freshmen and *Macbeth* to seniors. Anything else is considered a lowering of standards that will produce someone other than an educated person.

But what is the relevance of these subjects to the ghetto? What is their meaning to the youth who lives in a world of drugs, hunger, and a broken family? Shakespeare and European history are subjects clearly foreign to him both literally and figuratively, forced upon him by the dominant culture. They tell him that his own environment and experiences are not important and that, in fact, his life is a series of obscenities ignored by the larger society lest they bring about public embarrassment. In ignoring the realities of the ghetto, the curricula of urban schools violate one of the most sacred pedagogical principles—that learning must be based on the real life interests and experiences of the student. Otherwise the student learns only through abstractions, in a language that has no meaning and is applicable in a world which does not exist for him.

The rationale for separate minority courses is unquestionable. There is strong evidence that a major deterrent to learning among all types of minority students is the negative self-image that such students often possess. Experienced observers have noted that minority students often perceive themselves as less capable than members of the white majority. The result is poor motivation or, as is more likely, lower expectations. Regardless of the precise causes, the effects are clear: students from the racial minorities enter school at a deficit and fall farther and farther behind their Caucasian contemporaries.[1]

There is considerable evidence that an improvement in student self-images can lead to greater academic achievement. Irwin Katz, for example, has found that when black pupils perceive a less-than-even chance for success, they will give little effort to educational tasks and will show no progress, even a regression. Katz summarizes the available research findings related to racially integrated settings as contributory to improving black self-perception and academic achievement.[2] Martin Deutsch reports that the self-image is not related to achievement for students in general but is strongly related to achievement for blacks. Furthermore, according to Deutsch, it appears that the schools are capable of effecting little change in self-attitudes after students reach about the fourth grade.[3]

The first spokesmen for "relevant" special courses were the black militants. They based their viewpoints on historical precedent, arguing that minority groups in this country had first "to get themselves together" before they could gain acceptance by and achieve equality with the majority group. They pointed to Irish and other ethnic organizations, such as the Sons of Italy, to illustrate how minority groups built their own pride through a modified form of self-imposed segregation before acceptance was gained. They maintained that separatism is necessary in the early stages when an ethnic group is attempting to gain equality.

The speed with which school boards, boards of regents, faculty curriculum committees, and statewide coordinating councils of higher education have responded to these demands for new courses should gratify critics who have condemned education as an immovable object. But what have been the consequences of these special courses and what likelihood is there that they will achieve their intended goals?

As a practical consideration, separate courses have proven to be a strain on the financial and personnel resources of urban school systems. Such courses are expensive operations for several reasons. In many cities enrollments in these courses are very small, but in addition, these are courses added to a basic curriculum which therefore require additional staff members at the rate of approximately one extra teacher for every five classes. Furthermore, there are few people expert in these special areas although more and more college students, who are potential teachers, are registering in minority studies programs. At the present time, teachers of special courses are often merely individuals who have expressed interest in teaching such courses. The full cost of such courses is being felt in cities where other minority groups have followed the lead of black members of the community in requesting courses in brown history and literature, Indian history and literature, and Puerto Rican history and literature.

At this point, certain questions must be asked. What justification does a school board have in denying courses to Puerto Ricans where they have granted courses to blacks? And where will it all end? Recently major efforts have been made in attempting to organize other ethnic minorities to press for the supposed advantages obtained by blacks through separate courses.[4] Even in districts not under severe budget strains, there must be some reasonable limit.

From the standpoint of minority groups themselves, an even more important consideration is that ethnic-studies courses designed to enhance minority self-images may well succeed in achieving their objective, but in so doing they could lead to undesirable outcomes as well. Separate courses have certain side effects that are particularly serious in the case of blacks, but which also affect other minority groups as well. Likewise, there are also unfavorable effects on the white majority. If there were no better means for accomplishing the legitimate objectives sought through special courses, it might be desirable to accept these side effects as well as the greater financial costs and other drawbacks that have been mentioned previously. But as the authors attempt to demonstrate, there *are* better means for accomplishing the objectives that are sought by minority groups. This is the most forceful argument against the concept of the special course.

The Undesirable Side Effects

The basic problem is that the curricula of the ghetto school must both preserve and cultivate the cultural heritage of minority children at the same time that it brings them successfully into a world that can satisfy their aspirations.

Relevance is not only to be found in the ghetto. Quite the contrary. Learning solely about the ghetto would deny students any chance for personal betterment. While being based on the life in the ghetto, education for the disadvantaged must be transferable to life in the larger world. It must provide the ghetto child with the tools and cultivate in him the attitudes that will enable him to live and to compete successfully in the world of technical and professional work, the conditions of which are set in part by large economic and social forces extending far beyond his home and neighborhood.

This is not to denigrate the great importance of home and neighborhood in the educational process—providing that proper steps are taken. These are first to provide textbooks and materials that have meaning to ghetto students and then, when basic skills such as reading and arithmetic have been established, to employ these skills in the comprehension of more abstract, external concepts. Learning is a complex process that develops step by step; it begins with the simple and proceeds to the more difficult.

Perhaps the most basic question regarding special courses is the utility, over the long run, of the knowledge gained. A leading member of the black community, Andrew F. Brimmer of the Board of Governors of the Federal Reserve System, recently made an aggressive attack against these courses as dysfunctional in that they take from the black student the time he so desperately needs in other courses in order to stay abreast of his advantaged classmates.[5] Many members of minority communities regretfully acknowledge that the American society is and is going to remain a white middle-class culture and economy. The skills needed by minority students are those that will be of use in this culture. Many minority leaders recognize a clear need to build a self-image but not at the cost of mathematics, English, and reading.

The minority student must be aware that underlying our society are certain broad cultural assumptions that can only be ignored at great risk. While minority groups *must* be guaranteed their rights in society, they should also learn to accept other social systems. For example, the strong anti-Semitic note in some black-power statements has certainly dismayed many people.

The ultimate effect of special courses for a particular minority group is to further segregation and ultimately to further separatism. In separate courses, the student clientele comes predominantly from the minority group for whom the course was designed. (In some cases militants have attempted to bar white students from the black studies classroom.) An equally disturbing outcome of separate courses is that members of the white majority—the group that needs most to understand and to appreciate the contributions of minority groups—remain almost totally ignorant on these matters since they usually elect not to take these courses.

There is little hope for curing the racism endemic in this country until people generally become aware of and acknowledge their affliction. Whites fail to realize that any attitudinal reservation resulting from color, let alone any outright restriction, will clearly be perceived as racism by those discriminated against. How many whites, for example, recognize that it is blatant racism to hold a negative attitude about interracial marriage? Skin color, after all, is the simple and single determinant of that view. This is no less racism than is denying jobs or equal education on the basis of race; yet, although most of us hold this negative view, few recognize it as racism.

Most of us likewise fail to realize that what we intend is far less important than what someone else perceives. The use of phraseology offensive to a minority person may be considered inconsequential by the individual who did not intend to offend anyone. However, the recipient is rarely so philosophic.

Being a conservative force in our society, teachers reflect this racism in the classroom. Basic cultural differences are not tolerated, much less accepted and, even though racism may not be overtly expressed, it is an implicit element of the school milieu. Student grouping on the basis of tests having a built-in cultural bias leads to segregation even within integrated schools. Verbal behavior acceptable in the student's culture is penalized. Middle-class dress codes are rigidly enforced. Boisterous behavior common among poverty peoples is treated punitively. This rigidity inhibits both the teacher's and the student's understanding and acceptance of the other's different viewpoints. Student and teacher should be able to work together without forsaking basic cultural values instead of placing these values in conflict.

Thus, while minority studies may help in dealing with the immediate situation in terms of improving self-images, the pathology lies within the white community. It is there that we must place our greatest efforts.

An Alternate Strategy

We are led to two conclusions: we must integrate history and social studies and we must pluralize the culture of our schools. History must be accurate, factual, and representative; and teachers must be able to function in the mode of the several different cultures represented in their classrooms. It must be recognized that African geography and history, for example, are no less defensible areas of inquiry than are European studies. That we emphasize Europe over Asia, South America, and Africa is clearly because for most of us our ancestral ties are there. Similarly, we should identify and accentuate the African and Mexican heritages of other sizable segments of our society. Students must learn that differences between cultures are not "good" or "bad" but different ways of living, each of which has certain outcomes in terms of how people behave.*

---

*A simple example of a deeply ingrained value will easily illustrate this point. Cleanliness is a white middle-class value, dating back at least to the Victorian era. It is a value not held in such high esteem by various ethnic minorities in this country nor by majorities in many other countries. Yet

(footnote continued on next page)

The incorporation of minority studies into existing courses encourages integration and thwarts separatism by simple definition. Such courses would not be attended primarily by minority group members; all students would be in classrooms integrated as fully as the school itself is integrated. An important corollary would be that white students, who need to be informed about the contributions of minority groups, would gain this much needed knowledge. By integrating minority studies into existing courses, the artificial—even patronizing—nature of separate courses would be overcome. Both minority and majority students would begin to realize that minority contributions to society, when placed in the larger setting, are in fact very real and significant ones.

Imagine the effects upon a black student who learns of the contributions of John Swain, James P. Beckwourth, and Booker T. Washington in the context of a regular course as contrasted with the effects produced by the same information in a specially contrived course. Observers of comparative effects in integrated classrooms have noted that pride and an improvement in self-image are more likely to emerge when others are aware of the major contributions made by one's ethnic group rather than when these realizations are unshared. The emotional reaction of minority group members is, "See, members of my race are not so inferior as you (and I) thought. We too have made significant contributions to the development of this state or country." Elementary school principals in the Southwest, for example, have noticed a visible increase in the pride of Spanish-

---

our attitude about anyone who is not "clean" is so deeply imbedded in each of us that we cannot be objective about a person who does not meet our standards of cleanliness. Our media, especially through advertisements, transmit this point all too poignantly to minority groups. Imagine the effect upon small children who are told by society that they are dirty and offensive. We sometimes argue on a more rational basis that to be clean is healthy; whatever the merits of this proposition, Americans may indeed be an over-washed people from a health standpoint.

surnamed students when reports are given of the important contributions made by Mexican-Americans in the development of southwestern culture.

At the same time it is recognized that in many cities, where polarization of the races has been extensive, there is little likelihood that special courses already in being will be eliminated. The black leadership would be unlikely to surrender what they consider an important gain, and it is doubtful that they would be willing to accept on faith the alternatives suggested in this chapter. In other cities, where separate courses have not yet been demanded, the chances for the acceptance of practical alternatives remain excellent. As the successes of these alternatives become obvious, blacks in the more polarized communities will be able to observe the merits of these alternative actions. They should then be more willing to accept other options for improving self-images and for building cultural values.

Although temporarily it may be necessary to accept separate courses in certain communities, these situations should by no means be viewed as hopeless. Rather, the strategy must be different, and the timetable of events must vary with the local, social, and psychological situation of blacks and other minorities. The ultimate goal will be to eliminate separate courses for ethnic groups wherever they presently exist and to substitute a plan which reduces the negative features of separate courses.

However, all the arguments to this point are of no consequence if curriculum decision makers do not establish some priorities as to what must be included or excluded from the general curriculum and from individual course guidelines. Without such guidelines, we fall into a "creeping" curriculum that grows without direction or meaning. As we have noted, many cities now have extensive black-studies programs in progress. They have been and still are the catalysts for action on many fronts to establish the integration of subject matter.

Without such action, it is doubtful that there would have been much public pressure for the proper blending of subject matter and for a more equal racial treatment in the history texts. Factual, integrated history and social studies should replace curricula now in existence. This must have a high priority.

Pluralism, Assimilation, and Local Bias

History courses are generally the first area to gain minority-group attention. Unbiased history has been an elusive quest in American education. It is not difficult to make the argument that history, as presented in public school texts, is not history but a mythology developed for the express purpose of making history "more interesting." Battles, great historical figures, conflict, and strife are certainly more exciting than the slow progression of daily events that have shaped our society.

To be sure, our history will never—nor should it ever—be devoid of heroism and passions; there is much of this in our true heritage. But it is always worthwhile to ask whether heroes are made by their times or by historians attempting to capture an audience. One might ask how much mis-education we are promoting when we present an "enhanced" version of history to public school students. What images do we create when we emphasize and glorify the contributions of the predominant culture or representative members of that culture?

Actually, except perhaps in the pre-Colonial era, this country has never had a single basic culture. Not only were there enormous cultural differences between the American natives and the Europeans who colonized the country but there were also considerable differences between the various groups of Europeans themselves. These many diversities later helped to produce the different cultures of the Middle Atlantic states, for example, and the Southwest.

Nevertheless, cultural pluralism has never been presented in the public schools as a desirable social end. We have always advocated cultural assimilation rather than cultural pluralism, and the history textbooks have been distorted, however covertly, by this bias. By such phrases as "the great melting pot," the message has been carried to students that oneness in cultural values has been the goal of the American people. We idealized the European immigrants of the nineteenth century as persons attempting to become rapidly "Americanized." These recent immigrants who struggled in night school to learn the English language were glorified as persons with the true American spirit, the people who were seeking to overcome their European culture in order to become what everyone should want to become—a true American. The refusal to accept cultural pluralism has contributed to the basic racism that exists in white America.

The slanting of history to suit local biases has a long history of its own. Compare, for example, the content of Civil War history as taught in Alabama with the content as taught in Ohio. Or compare the textbook biographies of George Washington with the narratives of informed blacks who are aware of his extensive slaveholdings. Consider, too, the varying perspectives of the colonizer and the colonized. Surely there is a vast difference in the views of the British Empire held by British nationalists and by black Rhodesians; similarly the Alamo as glorified by Texans is seen in a different light by Mexican-Americans of the Southwest. Nor should it be forgotten that the American Indians, who were the victims of genocide, take quite a different view of this country's westward expansion from that held by the majority of Americans. As one reads American history texts, it becomes very clear that our history is to a considerable extent a collection of bits of biased reporting.

S. Samuel Shermis of Purdue University's Department of Education has identified with unusual insight some myths that delude history teachers, who in turn perpetuate these myths in the classroom. Following is Shermis' list of six such myths with his tart comments on each one.[6]

1. *There exists an entity called history.* There is . . . no such thing as history. There are only historical interpretations created by persons who have been labeled historians. What these interpretations are, of course, depend upon the given historian, his conception of philosophy, the time in which he wrote, and the prevailing notion of the structure alleged to be descriptive of his efforts . . . .

2. *History is, somehow, bound up with being a good citizen.* Mental discipline has been out of fashion for some years now, and we rarely hear anyone say that history trains the mind. Further, the argument that history is a sine qua non for a cultured man sounds a bit too aristocratic. Therefore, the familiar claim is that history is needed for the "training" of "good citizens." History, the story goes, is a record of the past, and we must study the past to make the right decisions in the future. This argument may not be invalid. I do not know.

3. *Students really can't think about history until they first have the facts.* While it is perfectly true that critical thinking does not take place in a vacuum, the notion that students must first be "given" the facts and then, at some distant time in the future, they will "think" about these facts is both a cover-up and a perversion of pedagogy. The entire process of problem sensing, problem formulating, data gathering and analysis, and confirming is called thinking. It is a serious error to separate facts from the other elements of thought. . . .

4. *History means diplomatic, political, and military history.* All teachers talk about making their subject interesting. What this means precisely is never clear. However, it could be interpreted to mean that the teachers would select certain aspects of the field that would likely hold interest for students. For history teachers such topics might consist of the development of technology or weaponry, the history of such cultural institutions as alcohol, the impact of French art in the nineteenth century, the rise of the city and attendant problems, the history of immigration, changes in American taste—or dozens of other legitimate historical subjects. But the practice is for history teachers to ignore what is not in the textbook, insisting on ritualistic coverage of prescribed information and then wondering why students don't give a damn. . . .

5. *It is possible to use history as a means of nationalistic indoctrination and also be scholarly.* There are two aspects of the history-cum-patriotism approach. The first emphasized the innocence and purity of our motives. Thus American blood was shed on American soil, we had only the noblest motives in entering World War I on the Allies' side, there was nothing really wrong with Black Jack Pershing's pursuing Pancho Villa into Mexico, and probably TR was right: God's will dictated our settling the continent from coast to coast, the Gadsden Purchase included. Along with the myth of our innocence is the belief in the depravity or inferiority of everyone else. The Japanese treacherously bombed Pearl Harbor, South Americans amuse themselves by holding scheduled revolutions, the Balkans are to be pitied for their fragmentation and silly nationalism, and the Russians are, always and forever, in the wrong. . . .

6. *The final myth is that the only conceivable way of teaching history is to begin with 1607 and work your way up to the present (or at least until Franklin Roosevelt's second term).* The trouble with this description is not that it is a sarcastic exaggeration, but that it is not. History classes do begin with the Colonial period, they do work their way inexorably forward, and the teacher rarely has time to deal with the last twenty years. Why history must be taught as undeviating, chronological progression is not clear. . . .

It can be argued that publishing companies must bear some of the blame for this distortion of history, with its convenient oversights. Publishers have not taken the initiative toward objectivity. However, publishing companies, like most other enterprises, respond to demands from their clientele—in this case the American public and the professional educators. A realistic history that takes a scholarly view of American history has not been demanded by American citizens and educators until recently, and then only in isolated cases. In those states having textbook committees, and in separate school districts of other states, there are now some demands for a fairer treatment of minority group contributions. This movement is in full motion—although, to be sure, the vast majority of textbooks presently in use do not contain this fairer treatment.*

New Models and Techniques

How is this process to be accomplished more speedily and thoroughly? Shermis offers a very interesting and useful model for change when he says, "Recent curriculum reforms have suggested that there are other and much more effective ways of teaching history." During the decade following Sputnik, science teachers in high schools and elementary schools were largely retrained, and science curricula were rewritten and revised in American public schools. This would seem a viable model for the sweeping changes in history, social studies, and literature that are advocated.

Curricula could be rewritten by bringing together subject experts and curriculum specialists to prepare textbook units and outlines, just as our leading scientists rewrote the science courses from the elementary classrooms through high school physics and chemistry. Scholars in all fields relating to the social studies should be retained under contract to provide a con-

----

*Some publishers of the new texts are also providing in-service training for teachers who will be using their texts. Whether this is merely a promotional device or a genuine attempt by publishers to encourage impartiality is beside the point. Free enterprise can work both ways.

tinuous check on written material for accuracy and perspective. Curriculum specialists, child development and reading specialists, classroom teachers, and students should be involved in material preparation.

The materials developed from such programs should, of course, be carefully evaluated, modified, and disseminated to the schools. This dissemination should be accompanied by in-service teacher training, and all feasible steps should be taken to insure their designated use. In-service programs, sponsored by school districts, are becoming ever more popular with administrators and teachers alike. These workshops provide special training in new techniques and methods and are of interest to the individual school district. Academic credit earned by attendance at these workshops is generally applicable to teacher credential renewal and to improved placement on salary schedules. In these ways, both parties—the school district and individual teachers—can benefit. By capitalizing on such precedents developed by the science institutes, we can greatly increase our effectiveness and efficiency in the social studies field.

Because of the far-reaching implications of a sweeping reform of curricula in history and social studies involving changes of behavior and of attitude toward minorities on the part of teachers, of equal necessity is a sweeping reform of teacher training extending back to teacher-training institutes. Again, there are suggestive models and techniques available for adaptation to this purpose.*

In the area of teacher-preparation programs, the Teacher Corps has done much to conceptualize and develop specific

---

*For still another model of a new kind of teacher-education institution—the Education Professions Institute (EPI), incorporating a large degree of local community control—see chapter by James C. Stone, "Training Teachers of the Disadvantaged: Blueprint for a Breakthrough," in *Resources for Urban Schools: Better Use and Balance*, the second volume in the CED Series on Urban Education.

teacher-training models. These models can be usefully applied to problems raised in this chapter. They are being implemented at the various colleges and universities that designed the programs. Human-relations training, competency based education, the role of the teacher as innovator, community development, and many other potential subjects are considered within these models. The resulting programs should produce teachers with a considerably different viewpoint and with a new set of classroom skills that should greatly increase teaching effectiveness.

Training that adapts teachers to other cultures is long overdue and will be well received by teachers. That teachers will be receptive to better preparation for working with minority groups is often overlooked. But it can be assumed that many teachers enter the profession not for monetary reasons but for personal satisfaction. They want to know how to relate to their students, how to gain their favor, even how to be loved by them. For many, this was the original reason for their professional choice. Most teachers are exasperated and even mystified when they are unable to gain the respect of minority students. With the teacher shortage all but ended and college budgets tightening, this would seem a logical time for a general reconsideration of all teacher-education programs.

For many years organizations such as the Peace Corps, which operate in foreign countries with markedly different cultures from ours, were dismayed to find that people newly posted abroad went into a state of shock. Nothing the newcomers did, or attempted to do, worked. They could not depend on any of the familiar guidelines that had existed at home. The world became a gray maze of frustration, mistakes, hurt feelings, and low productivity. These symptoms sound very familiar to those experienced by middle-class student teachers attempting to teach in schools with poverty or black populations; cultural shock is a frequently appearing phenomenon.

The training techniques developed for the Peace Corps are based on the premise that if the trainee is to achieve cross-cultural understanding, he must have an awareness of (1) the culture-bound assumptions that guide his thinking and actions, and (2) the assumptions that guide the thinking and actions of members of the second culture. These methods and materials could easily be adapted by teacher-training institutes to develop in prospective teachers the ability to understand and to work within the culture of our various minority groups. The materials would also promote considerable acceptance of cultural differences and would allow teachers to develop the skills needed to convey this attitude to their students.

Organizational Changes in the Schools

School administrators report little reluctance on the part of teachers to include minority contributions and to use ethnic studies bibliographies, audiovisual catalogs, and supplementary texts. Yet administrators find that this does not bring about dramatic changes in course content. They seem unaware of the constant pressures of teaching twenty-five or thirty hours per week, not to mention preparations for several different courses and the deluge of papers to be corrected. The problem is a feeling of incompetence brought on by almost complete ignorance of minority history and literature and by the lack of time to assimilate new knowledge.

Teachers generally seem most willing to teach about minority groups if they possess the necessary information. As mentioned earlier, teachers should be subsidized to attend institutes and summer workshops conducted by persons knowledgeable in minority studies. Without this supplementary education, there is unlikely to be effective treatment of minority contributions even when teachers are anxious to give them their proper place.

Techniques would have to be employed to make sure that teachers give more than lip service to these contributions. Once the administrative hierarchy and the school board have decided to adopt new programs, a complete sequence of curriculum development and in-service training should be planned and initiated. Members of the minority community must be included. The services of consultants from history, sociology, psychology, social psychology, and minority studies should be obtained, and condensations of their knowledge disseminated to all teachers and administrators who are involved.

Organizational training has as its focus the interpersonal skills, the group membership skills, and the problem-solving skills of individual staff members and natural organizational groups (such as departments or administrative cabinets). Over-all goals include the organization's ability to sense and adapt to its environment, as well as to achieve maximal utilization of resources. While these are not easy goals to attain, they can be reached; research in organizational training so indicates.[7] Furthermore, research reveals an accompanying increased sharing of ideas among teachers, an increased willingness to deal openly and constructively with conflict, and a transfer of skills to the classroom.[8]

Wherever such changes are attempted in methods of training, all school staff members should be involved. If principals and supervisors are to be adequately prepared to fulfill their roles, they must also be completely familiar and at ease with the materials and techniques being used in the classroom. Organizational training, as developed by the University of Oregon's Center for the Advanced Study of Educational Administration and by the Cooperative Project for Education Development (National Training Laboratories), should be considered essential in the development of the working ability of individual school faculties. These programs have proven their effectiveness in promoting the school staff's ability to work together to solve common problems and to set and achieve organization level goals. These programs also promote the restructuring of roles and relations within the staff for more effective utilization of abilities of staff and students.

If all these methods, new materials, and newly developed techniques were to be employed by the public schools and teacher-training institutes, it would be possible to achieve the two goals of curriculum integration and cultural pluralism. But educators must ask themselves if they are sufficiently committed to these goals to expend monies and energy toward their achievement.

Proponents of separate courses might well raise legitimate questions about the safeguards for insuring proper attention to minority group contributions in subject integrated courses. It in doubtful that new texts and reports from principals and teachers will be sufficient to give adequate reassurance to members of the minority community. However, there are several devices and techniques that could be utilized to give reasonable assurance for fair treatment, providing they are properly implemented.

School advisory boards are becoming quite common in many minority neighborhoods, and they should be established more widely; these could serve as the watchdogs over integrated history and literature courses. These committees would be involved in the employment of teachers and in any important curriculum decision; they could question applicants regarding their commitment to integrated course offerings. Almost any reasonable safeguard requested by the community should be accepted by educational leaders who recognize a need for alternatives to special courses.

The schools are certainly one area in which the leadership must do more than preach democracy; they must *practice* democracy. The public schools are perhaps the single remaining American institution that can be directly responsive to the people. As governments at all levels have expanded, the American educational system has retained wide acceptance as the one institution that can promote social equalization. From the days of the one-room rural school, public education has been the great hope of those seeking upward mobility. Though the public schools have been responsive to the local community, this responsiveness has declined as school districts have increased in size. The schools must return to their function of serving *all* the people. Through responsiveness to ethnic minorities, the schools can demonstrate that these groups do have a say in determining their personal destinies.

6. The Special Education Problems of the Mexican-Americans

Clark S. Knowlton

Not only has the American school system failed to educate Mexican-American children but likewise has closed the doors of social and economic opportunity in their faces. The school system has hampered their adjustment to Anglo-American society. It has damaged their identity, created feelings of inferiority, inadequacy, self-rejection, and group rejection. And it is now partially responsible for the constantly increasing unrest and tensions among the Mexican-American student population.

Unfortunately, the Mexican-Americans have been little studied. No comprehensive history had been written of the Mexican-Americans in the United States. A few sporadic studies of villages, neighborhoods, and communities exist; most of these by now are badly dated. Little attention has been paid to Mexican-American migration patterns, to the socio-economic conditions in which they live, and to the phenomena of culture contacts along the Mexican-American border.[1]

The sociological and economic problems presented by this rejected group of people transcends regional boundaries. Since the turn of the century, migratory currents have carried large numbers of Mexican-Americans to the major metropolitan centers of the Midwest, the Northwest, the Pacific Coast, and the Rocky Mountains. The industrial centers of the Midwest, such as Chicago, Detroit, Kansas City, and Flint, have large and growing Mexican-American settlements. The census takers of 1970 may well discover that the states of Illinois and Michigan have the largest Mexican-American populations in the nation outside the Southwest.*

A brief selection from among the scattered data that are available suggests the deplorable state of education for the Mexican-Americans.

In 1960, the median year of schooling completed by the Mexican-Americans in the Southwest was 7.1 years. For the Anglo-Americans, it was 12.1 years, and for the nonwhites (primarily American Indians in this region) it was 7.0 years.[2]

A study by scholars at the University of Texas in 1960 found 708,238 Mexican-American children and young people of school age resident in the state. There were 424,308 children between the ages of five and fifteen, of whom 20 per cent were not enrolled in the schools. There were 99,902 young people in the sixteen-to-nineteen age group, and of these 44 per cent were not enrolled.[3]

A similar study in California in the same year found that over 50 per cent of the men and almost 50 per cent of the

---

*A regular migratory current has come into existence. Because of high fertility rates, declining mortality, drought and soil erosion, a growing shortage of farmland, and the closing of exhausted mines in northern Mexico, Mexican nationals move toward the American border to cross into the United States. Their presence depresses the economic structure in the Southwest. Unable to earn a decent living there, the Mexican-Americans move in increasing numbers to the industrial and commerical centers of the Midwest and other regions. Their place in the Southwest is filled by the constant migration from Mexico. The poorly educated Mexican-American product of southwestern schools tends to exacerbate the difficult social problems of the northern cities, swelling welfare rolls, increasing unemployment and ethnic conflicts, and presenting the problem of absorbing large numbers of poorly skilled young workers into the economic structure. The political and economic leaders of the regions thus have a direct interest in the quality of southwestern schools. Furthermore, the general problems discussed in this chapter apply also to the school districts of the Midwest and its neighbors.

women among the Mexican-Americans had not gone beyond the eighth grade level. The comparable figures for the general population fourteen years of age or over was 27 per cent for the males and 25 per cent for the females.[4]

In the Denver public schools, 12 per cent of the Mexican-Americans of school age had dropped out of school compared to only 9 per cent in the general population.[5]

Officials of the Salt Lake City school system estimate that 67 per cent of all Mexican-American students drop out before finishing high school.[6]

There have been most unfortunate consequences from the neglect of Mexican-American studies. Not the least of these is a deplorable lack of knowledge among Anglo-American professionals, scholars, administrators, and planners about the culture, history, values, diversity, socioeconomic conditions, and current trends among the Mexican-Americans. Data essential for the development of comprehensive programs designed to improve existing conditions among the Mexican-Americans are not obtainable. Because of this lack, many government programs expending millions of dollars in the Southwest have either failed or have not had the success that their originators and administrators had hoped for.[7]

Many worthy projects in the Southwest have been aborted by a breakdown in communication, inability to agree on definitions of problems or priority of needs, conflicts over relevance, failure to coordinate private and public agencies, and rivalry between various government departments. The dangerous assumption that successful programs among blacks and Indians should succeed equally well among the Mexican-Americans, or that programs that have worked well with one Mexican-American group should succeed with other Mexican-American groups, still plagues Anglo-American planners and administrators in the fields of education, economics, community development, political organization, and social action.[8]

Although many Mexican-Americans feel that they have

been surveyed to death, a fundamental need exists for a good social history of the Mexican-American people. Also needed is a series of studies on villages and urban neighborhoods across the Southwest and Rocky Mountains to provide a social baseline against which future studies can be compared. Research on regional cultural differences, migration patterns, acculturation and culture contacts along the border, the changing family system, and the varying patterns of superordination-subordination would be extremely useful.

The complexity of Mexican-American history, internal groupings, and relationships with the dominant Anglo-American group is far greater than the most sympathetic observer is apt to realize. Mexican-Americans differ significantly in respect to their dialect of Spanish and the amount of English they utilize; their history, length of residence in the United States, and rural or urban residence; their racial composition, ethnic identification, degree of acculturation and values. Thus the rural Spanish-speaking people of northern New Mexico are quite different from the urban slum dwellers of San Antonio, who in turn vary from the Mexican-American inhabitants of Los Angeles. Amazing differences between distinctive Mexican-American groups can be found within the limits of a single county, such as El Paso county in Texas, where rural village people who have been in the Southwest before the American occupation live not far from recent immigrants from Mexico.

In this chapter an effort is made to analyze the educational needs and problems of the Mexican-American people. The culture and history of the Mexican-Americans germane to an understanding of their educational situation are discussed first. This is followed by a description of the specific educational needs of Mexican-American children generally, with emphasis on the direful effects of poverty, bilingualism, and cultural conflict. The unique difficulties of the children of migrant farm workers and the village population of northern New Mexico and southern Colorado are examined in a final section.[9]

Regional and Cultural Differences

The existing cultural divergencies among the Mexican-Americans are dramatized by their inability to agree on a name by which they may be known to their fellow Americans. This lack of a consensus is a reflection of regional differences, the cultural isolation of groups of Mexican-Americans from other groups for different periods of time, and the varied patterns of discrimination and segregation in the Southwest.

When Anglo-Americans and Mexicans met in the Southwest, each viewed the other through lenses of stereotyped prejudices that had originated in the religious wars of Europe and in the prolonged conflicts between Spain and England for trade and territory in the New World. Hostility was inevitable. In every military, economic, and political confrontation between the two groups, the Anglo-Americans were the victors. The fundamental fact in Southwestern history was the American conquest of the Southwest in 1847: all succeeding developments in the relationships between Anglo-Americans and Mexican-Americans have been deeply influenced by this central event.[10]

Anglo-American prejudices were intensified by the events at the Alamo, the constant raiding across the Mexican-American border by both Anglo-Americans and Mexicans from the 1830's to the 1920's with a few interludes of peace, and the strong and persistent resistance of Mexican-Americans to Anglo-American culture, language, and dominance. The following statement by an Anglo-American rancher in New Mexico illustrates the typical Anglo-American attitude in the West around the turn of the century.

> Now the general management and running of the ranch, [the Bell Ranch in eastern San Miguel County, New Mexico] before the eastern company acquired it and brought Arthur Tisdeal from the Paloduro ranch in Texas to be general manager, the ranch had been in the hands of western men of the old stamp reared under the pioneer

principles. They believed in the strong arm and there doesn't appear to have been any attempt to get the settlers [Spanish-Americans] off of the grant other than by scaring them and doing them dirt whenever an opportunity showed up . . . . He [the new manager] did not have to the full the prejudice against Mexicans that prevailed almost universally among the cattlemen of the West. It characterized almost all western Americans. This attitude and state of feeling spread over the West from Texas along with the cattle business which originated there. Its roots were in the Alamo. For the Texan of those days, it is true even of the present generation, the memory of that spot with its record of Mexican savagery kept alive a never failing flame of hatred and contempt for everything Mexican. As a consequence, the range men of these times treated the entire Spanish-American people as if they had no rights at all, refused to have any social relations with them, although some were of proud Spanish blood, killed them, disposed them of their lands, scattering their sheep and drove off their cattle.[11]

Before World War I, the Spanish-speaking groups of the Southwest were known, except perhaps for some elements in New Mexico, as "Mexicans"; English-speaking residents, as "Americans". This dichotomy reflected both the reluctance of the Anglo-Americans to accept the Mexicans as actual or potential American citizens and the ambivalence of the Mexican-Americans toward Anglo-Americans. Patterns of discrimination and segregation gradually developed in the region after the American conquest in 1847. These patterns varied according to the political and economic strength of the Anglo-Americans and Mexican-Americans. Where the Mexican-Americans managed to maintain some degree of political and economic power, as in New Mexico and in the lower Rio Grande Valley, subtle forms of discrimination came into existence. Where they were not able to assert some small degree of influence—as in most of Texas, many border regions in Arizona, and in many counties in California—the Mexican-Americans were soon enmeshed in a system of segregation that often resembled that of the blacks in the South.[12]

The World War I marked a major turning point in southwestern history. Until then, small groups of Mexican-Americans all along the Rio Grande continued to dream of establishing a Southwest independent of Anglo-American control. However, the patriotic fervor of the war, the service of many Mexican-Americans in the military, the harsh repressive activities of Texas Rangers and other police forces in uprooting those defined as "seditious," the revolutionary chaos of Mexico, and the postwar boom in the Southwest reconciled the Mexican-Americans to their destiny as part of the United States.

The change in attitude among those once called "Mexicans" was marked by the emergence of names that played down any identification with Mexico. In New Mexico and southern Colorado, an area that had experienced several hundred years of Spanish rule and only forty years under the Mexican flag, the term Spanish-American emerged after World War I. By the end of the 1920's, it was accepted by the Spanish-speaking people of the area who desired to differentiate themselves from the poorly educated and unskilled Mexican rural workers who were moving into New Mexico after World War I. A curious aspect of the situation is that many Spanish-Americans who resent being called "Mexican" by the Anglo-Americans refer to themselves in private when speaking Spanish as "Mexicanos." "Hispano" is another term for the Spanish-Americans used by a restricted circle of university students and teachers.

As prejudices softened, during this same period Anglo-Americans in California, Arizona, and Texas began to call the more acculturated Mexican-Americans, who spoke English and who had achieved a respectable social and economic position, either "Spanish-American" or "Latin-American". As more and more Mexican-Americans moved up the socioeconomic ladder, the terms spread throughout the Southwest. They have now become the polite words used by the mass media and by Anglo-American speakers at civic functions when referring to the Spanish-speaking people. The terms never became acceptable to the masses of the poorer Mexican-Americans, who found them insulting to their Mexican heritage.

These two terms have become subtle tools in the hands of Anglo-Americans to encourage acculturation into Anglo-American culture and rejection of Mexico and the Mexican cultural heritage; to drive a wedge between recent Mexican immigrants and older groups of Mexican-Americans; and to isolate the middle-class Mexican-Americans from the poor masses, thus depriving the middle class of any possibility of leadership and the poor of effective leaders. In effect, the middle-class, socially mobile Mexican-Americans were placed in a position of dependency upon the Anglo-American establishment. In return for a tacit agreement not to challenge the status quo, middle-class Mexican-Americans were given a few public positions—devoid of any real power—in which they could shine in the public eye as examples of what their people could become by acculturating.

Two new names have come into prominence in the Southwest during the past decade. The term "Mexican-American" began to spread during the 1950's among high school and college students, young professionals, and businessmen. Its emergence indicates a growing identification with Mexican cultural heritage, the economic, political, and cultural achievements of modern Mexico having become a source of pride among the younger generation. Its use implies a rejection of facile anglicization.

"Chicano," an even newer term, originated in the urban slums of the Southwest. It is probably derived from the Spanish word Mexicano. Recently formed militant Mexican-American groups use it as a badge of militant identity.

Throughout the history of the Mexican-American people, the Indian element in Mexican-American genes, culture, and psychology have been ignored by both Mexican-Americans and Anglo-Americans. The word Indian in Spanish is a term of reproach and connotes a lack of culture, good manners, and refinement. Mexican-Americans familiar with the negative Anglo-American attitudes toward the Indian have been very reluctant to call attention to their own Indian heritage. Among middle-class Mexican-Americans, subtle color prejudices against the darker skin colors have come into being.

Even this is now changing. Militant Mexican-American youth groups are calling themselves "mestizos," the Spanish word used in Latin America to describe people of mixed blood. They are emphasizing Maya and Aztec achievements as part of their own heritage. They now speak of brown power and mestizo people, opposing the word "brown" to "black" for the Negro and "white" for the Anglo-Americans.

Every Anglo-American working with Mexican-Americans or Spanish-Americans must be acutely aware of the importance of names. No name is currently acceptable to all groups. Each term will be offensive to a certain number of people. The use of the wrong term will generate considerable personal hostility. In this chapter, the word Mexican-American will be used as it currently has the largest acceptance.

The New Currents

Before World War II, Mexican-Americans were quite isolated from the Anglo-American world. Living in rural villages, mining camps, ranches, and in urban slum neighborhoods, few had any social contacts with Anglo-Americans. The barriers of culture, language, and discrimination and segregation were so strong that few Mexican-Americans crossed them. Those that did were professionals, small businessmen, government employees, and labor organizers who were essential to the Anglo-American establishment. These Mexican-Americans, speaking both English and Spanish, possessing a knowledge of both Anglo-American and Mexican-American communities, were able to exploit the ignorance of each group about the other to their own personal advantage. Few of them were ever really trusted by the mass of unculturated Mexican-American people.

World War II brought significant changes for Mexican-Americans in the Southwest. Thousands of young Mexican-Americans were drafted. Although facing some problems because of language and culture conflicts, their combat record won for them considerable respect in the military services and at home. The veterans returned quite secure in their identification as Americans and oriented toward acculturation. Large numbers of Mexican-Americans enrolled in government training programs during the war. Upon completion of training, these workers and their families were transported to defense plants in the urban centers of the Pacific Coast, the Southwest, the Rocky Mountains, and the Midwest.

The new middle-class Mexican-Americans are struggling for acceptance into Anglo-American society. Their children are discouraged from speaking Spanish. They seek out Anglo friends and model their family life upon the middle-class Anglo-American nuclear family. Extremely self-conscious and easily wounded, they are moving away from the traditional Mexican-American culture toward an Anglo-American society not yet willing fully to accept them. As they move toward acculturation, they tend to become contemptuous of the poorer less acculturated Mexican-Americans, who in turn regard them with suspicion, envy, and resentment. Any agency head who assumes that any well-educated personally competent Mexican-American can work well with poor Mexican-Americans will often be disillusioned.

Until very recently the Mexican slum dwellers, workers,

and villagers have been quite passive in the face of discrimination and segregation. The reasons for this passivity are easy to trace. The traditional upper-class groups who might have provided leadership disappeared. Protest leaders were simply eliminated or forced to leave the region. Until very recently, very few Mexican-Americans spoke enough English or understood the political and social mechanisms of American society well enough to organize successfully. The veterans of World War II, who might have provided a strong focus for organization, were for the most part enchanted with their new opportunities. The coming of one immigrant wave after another prevented the formation of a cohesive minority. Finally, certain Mexican-American values have seriously handicapped organizational endeavors.

The situation is changing very rapidly. Most Anglo-Americans in the Southwest and in the nation are unaware of the extent to which unrest is spreading. The unrest, interestingly enough, has sunk deeper roots among the alienated rural migrant workers in California and Texas and among the small farmers of northern New Mexico than in other areas. It is only in the last five years that the wave of unrest has reached the college and high school students and the urban slum inhabitants.

The unrest has been triggered by growing bitterness over the continued loss of land and water rights in New Mexico and southern Colorado; the failure of government's war-against-poverty programs—which come in with the blare of trumpets and the arousal of massive aspirations—to eliminate poverty or to improve conditions for the majority, even though many individuals have been helped; the fallout from the black civil rights movement; influences from Anglo-American student dissident groups; the growing awareness of Mexican-American students of the traditions of the Mexican Revolution; a general disenchantment with Anglo-American culture; and the increasing impact of Anglo-American values and population in the Southwest.

New leaders have emerged from the farm workers and rural villagers—Reies Lopez Tijerina in New Mexico and Cesar Chavez in California. They are charismatic leaders who have shared the poverty, the discrimination, and the cultural isolation of their people. Poorly educated, unacculturated, indigenous leaders, they have the ability to voice the hopes, the resentments, the bitterness, and the needs of their people. Unfortunately, few of them have much knowledge of Anglo-American values or of the American political and economic systems. They are simply not able to bridge the gulf between the two societies. However, they have broken through the apathy, the hopelessness, and the cultural and political isolation of the rural Mexican-Americans. They have definitely altered the entire political situation of the Southwest. Even though they may fail, they are preparing the ground for a more capable and better prepared leadership that may come.

These new leaders are quite alienated from the partially acculturated middle-class Mexicans, many of whom resent the prominence of the new leaders and their followers. Many middle-class Mexican-Americans feel that the goals of the new leaders will threaten the hard won and still precarious social, economic, and political positions secured by the middle class. They are fearful of Anglo reactions and are being squeezed by a serious identity crisis that is forcing many of them to redefine their attitude toward their own people and their position in Anglo-American society. And, finally, these new leaders are tugging at the heartstrings of many middle-class Mexican-American young people, inspiring them to study Spanish intensively, to take a new hard look at Mexican and Southwestern history, and to reassess their Mexican heritage.

As far as one can ascertain in a rapidly changing situation, the demands that these leaders are formulating include: (1) an end to poverty, poor housing, malnutrition, lack of medical care, police brutality, and other grievances that concern all minorities; (2) an acceptance of the Spanish language and

Mexican-American culture; (3) control of all social institutions in Mexican-American neighborhoods and villages; (4) adequate political representation; (5) an end to discrimination and segregation; and (6) the return of alienated land and water rights. This latter demand has already brought violence to northern New Mexico and threatens violence in south Texas.

Whether the migrants now entering the urban centers of the Southwest and other regions come from Mexico or from the Southwest itself, most of them originate in rural villages. Their basic institutions or social systems—such as the extended patriarchal family, the patron-peon system, the village community system, and folk Catholicism—do not function well in an American urban setting. The majority of the Mexican-Americans are a preliterate, preindustrial people whose values, attitudes, social systems and work skills seriously handicap their adjustment to a rapidly changing, dynamic, urbanized industrial system.

Isolated on the American side of the border, their language and their culture both have suffered through an inability to draw nourishment from the vigorous cultural traditions of Latin America. Since the Anglo-American conquest of the Southwest, a cultural "tortilla curtain" has been erected along the Rio Grande. Contemptuous of Mexico, most Anglo-Americans associate it with prostitution, drugs, alcohol, and curios, items very much in demand by Anglo-Americans. Anglo-Americans in the Southwest, the Pacific Coast, and the Rocky Mountains are as unfamiliar with Mexican art, literature, philosophy, history, culture, and intellectual life as they are with that of Afghanistan. Until very recently, few universities in the region, with the exception of the University of Texas, demonstrated much interest in the neighboring country.

Few Anglo-American intellectuals, writers, and scholars in the Southwest, the Pacific Coast, and the Rocky Mountain states have shown interest in Mexican-American history and culture until the last several years. School textbooks have ignored the subjects. Both have been excluded from the public school curriculum. Where today they are being introduced into universities and high schools, it is not because of any real interest among Anglo-Americans but because of the growing strength of militant Mexican-American student organizations.

As has been mentioned, not a single comprehensive history of the Mexican-American people exists. No regional, community, or local histories can be found. Until very recently, no periodical devoted to Mexican-American history and culture was published, nor was there a Spanish-language press devoted to popular publications. Mexican-Americans writing in Spanish had to seek publishers in Latin America. Few if any Spanish-language books or intellectual and scholarly journals have circulated in the region. Although many Spanish-language newspapers existed in the late nineteenth century, their number has steadily diminished.

Poverty and Malnutrition

The educational needs and problems of Mexican-Americans vary according to the many differing local, class, and other factors that have been described. For example, the educational problems of rural migrant farm children on the move from April to November differ substantially from those of a stable population. An educational program planned for the culturally isolated rural village children of northern New Mexico and southern Colorado would have to vary from programs designed for urban slum children in El Paso, San Antonio, Albuquerque, Los Angeles, or Tucson. The Mexican-American children of neighborhoods where little Spanish is spoken would have different needs from those where little English is spoken.

However, there are certain educational needs and problems common to the majority of Mexican-American children. In this category are the problems related to poverty, language and culture conflicts, curriculum, teaching materials, counseling, teacher selection and training, discrimination and segregation. Foremost among these, simply enough, is the stark fact of extreme poverty and the crushing burden it imposes on the child.

Although few studies exist that measure poverty among Mexican-Americans, as a group they would be defined as poor by any economic index. Almost all of them earn less than $3,000 a year and in many areas less than $2,000. Large numbers subsist on $1,000 or even less a year. Wage levels throughout the Southwest for unskilled labor are at or even below subsistence levels because of the heavy pressure on wage levels exerted by constant Mexican immigration. Even though the income averages for Mexican-American residents in the Midwest, the Rocky Mountains, the Pacific Coast and the Northwest are considerably higher than those of the Southwest, they are still near the bottom for the states involved.[13]

Any observer walking through an average Mexican-American neighborhood can note the casual evidence of poverty such as deteriorated housing, poorly fed and dressed children, aging vehicles, and clusters of unemployed men and women. If he were to stop by a group of mothers and children, he could easily determine the existence of malnutrition by observing the pallor noticeable even in the brown skins, the unhealthy skin and flesh tone, the listlessness, the puffiness, the anemia, and the lip sores.

The first and most important characteristic of poverty among Mexican-American school children is malnutrition. Although statistics are lacking, it is my impression that in the counties along the Mexican border in Texas, New Mexico, Arizona, and California, as well as in northern New Mexico and southern Colorado, the majority of Mexican-American children living in migrant labor camps, rural villages, cattle ranches, and urban slums suffer from malnutrition that in some areas verges on starvation.

Disease and poor health are important by-products of poverty among the Mexican-Americans. Few have any access to modern medical care. Native healers are the local doctors and psychiatrists; they follow a variety of medical traditions supplemented by dosages of penicillin. Unrecognized and untreated anemia, venereal disease, and tuberculosis shadows the classroom. Wave after wave of infectious diseases such as measles, mumps, and chicken pox pass through the Mexican-American school population. Poliomyelitis is still a crippler in rural villages, migrant labor camps, and urban slums.

Toothache is regarded simply as one of the burdens to be endured by the poor. The nervous strain caused by toothache, pyorrhea, and lack of normal dental development troubles the learning process of Mexican-American children. Teachers noticing bad, untreated teeth are apt to blame the situation on laziness, parental unconcern, or poor personal habits—not realizing that adequate dental care either is unavailable or a luxury that poor Mexican-Americans cannot afford.

Unfortunately, few Anglo-American middle-class teachers and administrators staffing schools attended by poor Mexican-American children have any knowledge about the impact of poverty upon the learning process. Even though many sympathetic teachers and administrators build up funds to provide free clothing, glasses, and medical care, they are too embarrassed to confess that malnutrition is a serious problem in their schools. Having seldom experienced poverty or hunger, they are not psychologically equipped to understand what malnutrition and poverty can do to the health, welfare, and learning ability of children.

Mexican-Americans are a proud people. Many children are not sent to school because the family cannot afford to buy them school clothing. Others drop out of school because they are humiliated and embarrassed by their clothing or because they do not have money for school activities. Junior high and high schools impose an especially heavy financial burden upon the poor. School fees and textbooks are quite often beyond the ability of many families to pay. Poor Mexican-American children seldom participate in athletics, bands, orchestras, drama, school clubs, and societies; yearbooks cost far too much for them to buy. Public schools may be public but they are not free.

At home, the schoolchild may sleep on the floor wrapped up in newspapers and torn blankets, and at best he will share room and bed with other members of his family. In winter his house is cold; and in summer, stifling. The noise level of conversation, radio, and television is high. There are few, if any, books, dictionaries, or newspapers in either Spanish or English in any homes. The child must struggle unaided with the English language and other school subjects; his parents can seldom help him. The attractions of the street are numerous. If a boy is near adolescence, his parents and his friends alike would think it odd for him to spend much time at home. A teacher who requires homework from poor Mexican-American children is asking for the impossible unless provisions are made for the child to do the work at school.

Clearly, the alleviation of these many problems afflicting the Mexican-Americans can only come about through the eradication of poverty in this country. However, much can be done on a local level to improve conditions for Mexican-American schoolchildren—if programs are pursued rigorously and with regard for their special situation and their sensitivities.

School districts can reduce the impact of malnutrition among Mexican-American school children by providing free breakfasts, lunches, and after-school snacks. Many school districts with large populations of poor Mexican-American children do not provide school lunches. Many that do, require work from students who receive free lunches, demand that parents pass a means test, or give tokens of different color to recipients of free lunches from those sold to more affluent students. The need to maintain self-respect causes large numbers of Mexican-American students in need to refuse to participate in free-lunch programs. Anglo-American school personnel find it difficult to give gracefully. In schools located in poor neighborhoods, free food should be provided to all students as a right. In middle-class schools with numbers of poor children, the poor children should be given food in such a way that they cannot be identified by other students.

The same situation prevails in the distribution of clothing. In every poor Mexican-American neighborhood, schools and other institutions could open distribution centers for either the free distribution or the sale at very low prices of good clothing. In situations where parents lack income to buy clothing and free clothing is provided, it is essential that this be done under conditions that preserve the self-respect and pride of poor Mexican-American families.

The development of a network of free or extremely low-cost health clinics in poor Mexican-American neighborhoods is the only adequate method of improving health conditions among Mexican-American school children. Staffed by Spanish-speaking personnel, the clinics should be given the resources necessary to carry on an intensive public health and medical educational program among a population unfamiliar with the germ theory of disease. Until this is done, a free comprehensive medical and dental examination should be administered to all school children. The school districts should have the facilities to provide remedial surgery, glasses, hearing aids, and other health needs without cost to the students. The improvement of health conditions among the students would bring about a marked improvement in their academic performance.

Public schools should become *free* public schools. No public school district should be permitted to require money from students or parents for any reason. This single change would alone retain large numbers of Mexican-American students in the schools. It is not enough for the schools to state that they will excuse students from poor families from payment of school dues. The names of those excused always become public. Students are humiliated by the implied confession of poverty and many would rather drop out of school than request exclusion from fee payment.

Illiterate in Two Languages

The vast majority of Mexican-American children enter school from Spanish-speaking homes. They will know little English. They will never have had any intimate relationships with Anglo-American children of their own age. Anglo-American adults to the majority of these children are menacing figures represented by police, social workers, rent collectors, and storeowners. Unable to speak English, they will be placed in an English-language classroom staffed by English-speaking teachers who know little Spanish.[14] The result is what Sweetland has called "the most signal failure in American education."

The poorly-fed, poorly-dressed Mexican-American child enters a school that rejects his language and culture and thus rejects him. During the school day, if he is caught speaking Spanish—the only language that he knows—he is punished. In a strange tongue, whose concepts are alien to him, he must struggle to learn to read and to master such subject matter as arithmetic. Facing an impossible situation, he naturally falls behind the Anglo-American child, and the gap increases each year. Conditioned to failure, the Mexican-American child faces increasing frustration each year that he remains in school. Timid and fearful, he retreats into his own Spanish-language world; to protect himself from the harsh English-speaking world, he may erect psychological barriers that may not disappear in his lifetime. Sensing these barriers, teachers frequently react by rejecting the child or classifying him as a slow learner or mentally retarded.

Mexican-American children are often placed in catchall special programs that are actually terminal and shunt the child away from college entrance courses. These special programs, federally financed, are designed to provide a minimal high school education for children defined as unable to benefit from the regular college preparatory sequence. Teachers place children whom they cannot reach in these courses. Once a child is placed in these special programs, it is almost impossible to get him out because the high school secures additional federal funds by his being there. A Mexican-American child in these courses loses all hope; ridiculed by his peers, he struggles to leave school any way that he can.

The Mexican-American child not only must fight for survival in the toils of an alien language but is forced to take intelligence tests in which his language, culture, socioeconomic world, and life experiences all are against him. He may have fully as great an intellectual potential as the Anglo-American child, but he will frequently show up on the tests as a "low achiever" or "nonlearner," or as "mentally retarded."[15] The scores he receives hang like an albatross around his neck. They are used to assign him to school grades, to determine the attention devoted to him by his teachers, and the academic opportunities that may be provided him. These grades stereotype him in the eyes of Anglo-American administrators and teachers, and even in his own eyes. These administrators and teachers make it very clear that they expect little of him—and he manages to live up to their expectations.

As the Spanish-speaking child has seldom mastered the basic grammatical concepts of the Spanish language before he is forced to deal with English, he seldom learns either Spanish or English well. Almost any school can turn out children illiterate in one language, but the schools attended by Mexican-American children have the distinction of turning out children functionally illiterate in two languages. The child may come to speak Spanish better than English but read English better than Spanish —and not really communicate well in either language. Some children even seem to lose the ability to use Spanish while acquiring a poor quality English in the framework of Spanish pronunciation and grammar.*

The methods now used to teach English to non-English-speaking children in the majority of our school systems are completely out of date. The average English teacher teaches English to Spanish-speaking children the same way that she does to native English-speaking children. The result is that few Spanish-speaking children acquire an effective command of the English language. This method is completely contrary to all the basic principles of linguistics. Teachers should be specially trained in the new methods recently worked out for the teaching of English to non-English-speaking children and by the adoption of all the modern developments in electronic equipment and language laboratories. These methods are now being used in military establishments and in universities and colleges throughout the United States. Unfortunately, they have not yet been adopted on a large scale by elementary and secondary schools.

The basic goal of schools in the Spanish-speaking areas of the Southwest should be to produce students who can effectively speak, read, and write both Spanish and English and to comprehend both Spanish and Anglo cultural values. To achieve this,

---

*Bilingualism in the Southwest has been used as a convenient whipping boy to explain away the educational deficiencies of the Spanish-speaking children, and to obscure the fact that no equality of educational opportunity exists in the Southwest or in Texas. By pointing to bilingualism as the factor responsible for their educational deficiencies, one can then forget that the majority of Spanish-speaking children live in urban slums or in rural villages where the school buildings are poor, antiquated, or simply inadequate. Because of the lower taxing power of poverty areas, local teacher salaries are inadequate, the schools are sadly lacking in equipment, and only the basic core curriculum can be taught. A Spanish-speaking child in Mora or Penasco, in la Union or Anthony does not have the same educational opportunity as an Anglo child in Albuquerque, Carlsbad, or Roswell. Unfortunately, there is little realization in these larger urban centers that the products of the poorer slum and rural village schools will migrate to them in search of employment. As the migrants are not adequately prepared, they create serious economic and social problems that to a large degree could be averted if all children in the state were given equal educational opportunities.

both English and Spanish should be used as basic teaching languages. Many recent experiments have shown that children who master their native languages well can more efficiently learn another language than can children who have not completely learned their native languages.[16] Recent tests in Canada show that children who are bilingual when matched with monolingual children of the same socioeconomic backgrounds learn faster, progress at a more accelerated rate, and are more intellectually mature.[17]

Scattered school districts in Florida, New York, and in Laredo, Texas, are abandoning the older system of using English exclusively and are now teaching in both Spanish and in English. One school district near Miami, for example, is teaching all courses in Spanish in the morning and in English in the afternoon. In New York, Puerto Rican children are learning much faster through a bilingual approach than before. As a result of the new experiments in the use of Spanish, the state of Colorado has now set an example by repealing its law that English must be the only language of instruction. It is time that New Mexico and Texas followed this example. In both New Mexico and in Texas, state laws permit the experimental use of Spanish as a teaching language.[18]

To achieve the goals of bilingual education, it may be necessary to involve the Mexican-American child in the formal educational program at the early age of three or four. If, by the age of six or seven, a Mexican-American child could acquire the rudiments of literacy in both Spanish and English, the learning process would be enormously facilitated. Computerized, programmed courses; communication-systems analysis; modular instructional units; and other evolving educational systems may be used also to improve the learning environment of students. One further urgent need is additional research in the related variables involved in the learning process of bilingual Mexican-American children.

The Cultural Conflict

Mexican-American school children pass through their entire school careers, learning little if anything about their own history and culture. There is virtually nothing in their school experience or textbooks with which they can identify. The self-image of the children, already lacerated by the scarcely concealed contempt of so many of their teachers and Anglo-American classmates, is badly damaged by the overwhelming saturation in Anglo-American history and culture.

The impact of cultural conflicts upon the educational progress of the Mexican-American child is summarized by the statement of A. Bruce Gardner, Specialist in Foreign Languages with the U.S. Office of Education, at the Second Annual Conference of the Southwest Council of Foreign Language Teachers, November 13, 1964 at El Paso:

The greatest barrier to the Mexican-American child's scholastic achievement . . . is that the schools reflecting the dominant view of the dominant culture want that child to grow up as another Anglo. This he cannot do except by denying himself and his family and his forebears, a form of masochism which no society should demand of its children.[19]

Many children in an effort to salvage their self-respect drop out of school. Others turn to juvenile delinquency and crime against the Anglo-American world. And still others gradually adopt Anglo-American attitudes and come to reject themselves, their families, and their ethnic group. Anglo-American children who have never observed Mexican-Americans in any role except a subordinate one have their attitudes of contempt and superiority reinforced.

Whenever people of diverse ethnic, racial, or religious characteristics come into contact with each other, cultural conflicts are almost certainly inevitable. In a nation such as the United States, composed of immigrants from diverse parts of the world, these conflicts are more common than they would be in a more homogeneous society. Because of the potential threat of disunity, the cultural policy of the United States has been to emphasize the Americanization of immigrants. This policy requires that immigrants must divest themselves of their languages and cultures and put on new cultural clothes made in the United States.

The school has been a major instrument of this Americanization policy. Immigrant languages, cultures, and their contributions to the United States tend to be slighted by historians. Regardless of the heavy cultural, intellectual, social, or psychological price paid by the immigrants and their children, they have been for the most part Americanized. For many reasons, this policy has failed with the Mexican-Americans. The cultural and linguistic intolerance implied by this policy of Americanization has assisted in the educational retardation of this group and now along with other factors threatens the tranquility and prosperity of the Southwest and neighboring regions.

School curriculum in each of the states containing substantial numbers of Mexican-American children is standardized by (1) laws that require the schools to teach certain materials such as American history and forbid them to teach in languages other than English; (2) rules and regulations of regional accrediting associations; (3) the entrance requirements of state universities and colleges; (4) the educational philosophy of the dominant Anglo-American society as expressed by teachers, administrators, and members of boards of education.

Complaints about nonrepresentative textbooks, readers, and other instructional materials have been registered many times by Mexican-American leaders. Their most serious complaint is that local, regional, or national history textbooks either completely ignore the Mexican-Americans or that they reflect regional prejudices and biases against them. History courses are of fundamental importance. They serve as a mirror in which

individuals, ethnic groups, races, and political parties see themselves. Historians tend to stress ethnic and racial groups, the
historical experiences, the heroes, and the values that played
important roles, as defined by popular opinion, in the development of a nation. Groups defined in a negative way by historians suffer from lowered self-esteem, a poor image among
Anglo-Americans, and increased regional prejudice. History
ought to be written in such a way that a fair impartial
account is given of the experiences and contributions of all
ethnic and racial groups that have lived in the United States.

School readers and other instructional materials used to
teach English, mathematics, and other subjects in southwestern
schools are usually built around the cultural and social environment of the Anglo-American child. To redress this, special
programs have been designed to motivate and assist Mexican-
American students. A fundamental weakness of such programs
is that they have been devised by middle-class Anglo-American
educators; though often sympathetic to the educational needs of
Mexican-Americans, they have little knowledge by and large of
Mexican-American values and culture or of the Spanish language. Most of these programs have been designed within the
traditional educational philosophy of acculturation and assimilation of the Mexican-Americans into the dominant Anglo-
American society.

The majority of these new programs have focused upon
so-called cultural enrichment: smaller classes, better trained
teachers, remedial teaching of basic subjects, exposure of the
students to various types of careers, field trips to break down
cultural isolation, greater use of audiovisual techniques, more
liberal and varied use of textbooks and other types of teaching
materials, and the use of teacher aides (who may or may not be
of the same ethnic group as the students). These programs have
been of some assistance in improving the educational situation
of the Mexican-American, but they have not diminished the
extremely high dropout rate, overcome the problems of lan-

guage and culture conflicts, or met the physical needs of poor children.

A second basic problem with educational programs for the Mexican-Americans is caused by the tendency for Anglo-Americans to overgeneralize and oversimplify the formulation of such programs. The subtle but important cultural differences that separate one Mexican-American group from another are not known to Anglo-Americans and therefore tend to be ignored. Programs that seem to have some success with Spanish-speaking Cubans or Puerto Ricans in New York City and in Florida are hastily adopted for Mexican-American children—who find them absurd. Programs that improved educational performances in Los Angeles or in San Antonio are imported by school districts in other regions without any realization of the need to regionalize, modify, and adjust educational programs to the specific needs of local Mexican-American populations.

This is not to say that teaching materials from Mexico are not useful. As auxiliary materials they can be used to strengthen self- and group-respect and to broaden the cultural world of the Mexican-American child. Mexican histories, novels, paintings, and illustrations of Mexican scenery and cities can be fitted into normal school activities. It is recommended that units on Mexican and Mexican-American history, culture, and values be blended into the curriculum of elementary and secondary school curricula.* This blending should be done in such a way that these subjects seem like a natural part of the history and culture of the Southwest and of the United States rather than a lump of foreign matter.

---

*It is very difficult to provide adequate teaching materials on Mexican-American history and culture at the present time. As previously mentioned, very little material can be found in print. By supporting scholarship and research in this area, a foundation or university could help to fill the existing gap. Sponsorship of an intellectual journal in Mexican-American history and culture would be extremely useful in providing an intellectual forum in which scholars could discuss their findings. Such a journal could foster interest and concern in this whole area.

It would be helpful to introduce material on Anglo-American values, institutions, and social systems in social science and general citizenship courses in schools with many Mexican-American students. In general, they are as puzzled about Anglo-American society, as Anglo-Americans are about Mexican-American behavior. Courses of this nature need to be taught by sympathetic teachers who are aware of the problems of culture conflicts and who are familiar with both Anglo-American and Mexican-American culture.

Certain general recommendations can be made for the improvement of curricula and materials for the education of Mexican-American children. Very important among these is the introduction of teaching units on the history, culture, and historic contributions of the Mexican-Americans, as well as of similar units on the history and culture of Mexico and other Latin American countries and their relationships to the United States. There should be an elimination of the large number of openly or subtly biased textbooks and their replacement by a series of carefully developed books in both Spanish and English reflecting the world of Mexican-American children.

There should be a very heavy emphasis on the development of so-called culture-free testing instruments in both Spanish and English. Teachers should be carefully and rigorously trained in the evaluation of testing instruments, both oral as well as written. (Oral instruments may be more accurate in certain situations among Mexican-American students than written tests because of problems with written English.) There must be careful testing of those Mexican-American children who have been classified as either mentally or culturally retarded or who have been placed in special courses away from the mainstream of academic life. This testing must be done by educators who are bilingual and who have the ability to conduct intensive remedial courses for the correction of educational deficiencies among Mexican-American students.

Training and Recruiting Teachers

Most of the school personnel in the Southwest and West, where the majority of Mexican-American students are found, come from the Anglo-American middle class. They share a common middle-class Anglo-American value system that pervades the school system. These values are seldom articulated, questioned, or verbalized. They are simply taken for granted. School personnel are trained by university departments of education that are staffed by middle-class professors who also accept this value system. They may add to it certain ideas derived from the progressive school of education, such as permissiveness, openness, freedom from structure, accent on individuality, personal development, creativity, self-understanding, peer groups, and social mobility. But they have little knowledge of the culture, history, values, and living conditions of Mexican-Americans. As a group, the educators are singularly unprepared to assist or to motivate their Mexican-American students. Among them are also many prejudiced individuals who close the door of educational opportunity in eager Mexican-American faces.

Although the majority of young Mexican-Americans enrolled in colleges and universities major in education, they cannot find employment because of discrimination and prejudice in many school districts in New Mexico, Colorado, Arizona, and Texas. Because of an acute teacher shortage, the situation is far better in California. In many school districts Mexican-Americans are hired to teach Spanish but are not employed in other academic areas, the rationalization being that their "Mexican" accent will contaminate the accent of the children. And in still other districts, Mexican-American teachers are assigned to segregated Mexican-American schools and seldom appear in the Anglo-American schools in the same school districts.

Where they are hired, they often face a concealed salary

differential. That is, Mexican-Americans teaching the same subjects as Anglo-Americans, with the same academic qualifications, experience, and seniority, will be paid a lower salary than Anglo-American teachers. Few Mexican-American teachers are able to move up to higher salary brackets and more responsible school positions. Mexican-American teachers tend to be frozen into the lower salary levels and less important school assignments. Very often they face snubs and open harrassment by Anglo-American personnel who refuse to accept them as colleagues.

Prejudice has blocked the movement of Mexican-Americans into positions of counselors and principals. The El Paso school system is an excellent example. Over 60 per cent of the school children enrolled are Mexican-Americans. Up to 1968 there were only two Mexican-American counselors and two Mexican-American principals, both in charge of elementary schools. Very few Mexican-American names are found on the roster of the central school office personnel.

Many school districts rationalize their prejudice by saying that they cannot find either Mexican-American school personnel or qualified Mexican-Americans for higher positions. It is true that an acute shortage of Mexican-American teachers, counselors, and principals does exist; but the majority of school districts make no effort to recruit, to train, or to find qualified Mexican-Americans. They tend to recruit personnel in midwestern and southern states that export teachers rather than in states such as New Mexico and Texas that are turning out a trickle of Mexican-American teachers and administrative personnel.

The massive failure of school districts even to recognize, let alone resolve, the educational problems and needs of Mexican-American school children, is compounded by the prejudice, inertia, and rigidity of university and college departments of education. For the most part, they have failed to develop the courses, the workshops, and field assignments to acquaint their prospective teachers with Mexican-American history, culture, values, and unique educational needs and problems. For several decades educational pioneers have been urging the development of such training programs; yet it was not until militant Mexican-American protest groups, in and out of the universities, demanded such programs that universities and colleges began glacially to move. Even today, the majority of teachers graduating from departments of education in the Southwest, the Rocky Mountains, and the Pacific Coast receive no exposure to Mexican-American history or culture.

Much of the credit for what improvement has taken place in the schools of these regions can be traced to the personnel of the state departments of education, such as the Texas Educational Agency, that have hired Mexican-American teachers, principals, and counselors to assist and to advise them. Many of these departments have conducted experimental programs in bilingualism and development of teaching units in Mexican-American history, culture, and values. They have also disseminated materials; exerted pressures against reluctant school districts; financed special programs in many areas of ethnic and racial education; and endeavored to educate state legislators, school boards, principals, and teachers. Their efforts have been supported by the new federally financed regional educational laboratories set up to conduct educational research and develop new programs. Several of these laboratories, such as the ones in Austin and Albuquerque, have played important innovative roles in the educational world of the Southwest.

It would be unfair to imply that there is no progress at all. A small number of school districts in Arizona, California, Texas, and New Mexico are beginning to experiment with the use of Spanish as a teaching language and of English as a second language; the development of language laboratories; the accelerated use of Mexican-American teachers and teacher aides, team teaching, special neighborhood and home tutoring projects; and the utilization of exchange teachers from Latin America.

Unfortunately, progress has been very slow. Such experimental programs have met serious resistance from Anglo-American school personnel and from an Anglo-American community totally convinced of the values of monolingualism and acculturation of minority groups. Many in the schools view these programs as a personal threat to them as they do not speak Spanish and know so little about Mexican-Americans. Much of the resistence rests on a latent fear in the Southwest of being submerged in a rising sea of brown faces speaking Spanish. The schools are seen as fortresses defending the values of American democracy and the English language against insidious threats from beyond the border.

Few Mexican-American children receive any type of counseling in the public schools except in disciplinary matters. The majority of the counselors—and it should be kept in mind that a large number of poor school districts in the Southwest have no counselors—seldom speak Spanish or have any knowledge about the problems and needs of the Mexican-Americans. Others who are prejudiced treat these children with contempt and hostility. The reports of negative experiences with one counselor will spread rapidly and cause Mexican-American children to boycott all counselors. Few Mexican-American children will go to an Anglo-American for advice and assistance because of shyness, uncertainty, and fear of rebuff. Many of their problems have to do with family or poverty and therefore are not the kind that the average Anglo-American school counselor can solve.

What counseling the Mexican-American children receive is usually provided by some teacher defined by the children as friendly, sympathetic, and free from prejudice. Children will go for advice to a teacher in whom they have confidence. Unfortunately, many of these sympathetic teachers lack the knowledge about community agencies and educational opportunities to advise the students wisely.

This lack of counseling is very serious. The author of this paper spoke to forty Mexican-American high school seniors in

Salt Lake City about university opportunities. Of this group, two had received university scholarships as a result of proper counseling; thirty of them had had no contact with a counselor except on disciplinary matters. They were not aware of the scholarship programs of Utah universities. The lack of counseling had closed the doors of educational opportunity to them.

Two types of counselors are needed. They should be sympathetic to Mexican-Americans wherever possible. One type of counselor needed is the academic counselor who can provide assistance in traditional academic matters. The second type is the personal counselor who can assist Mexican-American students caught between two culture worlds about their personal problems. Properly trained Mexican-American counselor aides should be provided every counselor working with Mexican-American children. These aides can be used to secure data about the family and neighborhoods of the children, to provide liaison with social agencies such as welfare, juvenile courts, and even the police departments.

A number of actions must be taken at all levels to overhaul the entire process of recruiting and training teachers for Mexican-American students.

Every effort must be made by means of four-year scholarships and other inducements to recruit capable Mexican-American students into the teaching profession. Few Mexican-Americans graduate from high school and even fewer, for financial reasons, attend universities and colleges. School districts with substantial numbers of Mexican-American students should be required to hire proportionate percentages of Mexican-American teachers, counselors, principals, and educational staff or lose their federal subsidies. Schools with small numbers of Mexican-American students must employ Mexican-American teachers and counselors to serve as role models for Mexican-American students and perhaps to modify existing stereotypes about Mexican-Americans in the minds of the Anglo-American students and their parents.

The concept of Mexican-American paraprofessionals has not yet received widespread acceptance in southwestern schools. Large numbers of schools serving Mexican-American students utilize government funds to hire Anglo-American paraprofessionals who are relatives of school personnel or poor Anglo-Americans. Others tend to hire middle class Mexican-Americans who have little insight, rapport, or sympathy with poor Mexican-American children. An investigation into the misuse of federal funds appropriated to improve the educational opportunities for poor and for minority group children is long overdue in the Southwest, the Pacific Coast, and the Rocky Mountains. Every school serving Mexican-American children should utilize the services of trained Mexican-American teacher aides, counselor aides, and principal aides (for liaison with the Mexican-American neighborhoods). The school personnel and their dependent aides must be trained together as a team to insure the proper use of aides and to avoid role conflicts.

All school personnel teaching Mexican-Americans should be required to take in-service training in Mexican-American and Mexican history, culture and values; the techniques of teaching bilingual children and the Spanish language. Furthermore, mechanisms must be set up in all school systems to transfer out immediately any personnel defined as prejudiced. Mexican-American students are becoming increasingly sensitive to prejudiced teachers and are apt to react through walkouts, strikes, and even riots to their continued presence in the school systems. And, finally, the teaching and administrative staffs of schools in Mexican-American areas of poverty should be given a substantial salary advantage over the staffs of middle-class and suburban schools.

The process of teacher recruitment and training in university departments of education must be reorganized. Very few products of these departments, in my experience, are functionally able to work successfully with Mexican-American and Indian children. Special recruitment programs must be established to recruit prospective teacher candidates from the ranks of young people in the streets, young mothers on welfare, and even from the leadership of street gangs. These people may have the insight and the personal experience needed to turn them into very effective teachers. Mexican-American urban slums, rural villages, and migrant labor camps are filled with wasted talent. Perhaps the greatest indictment of the present social structure of the Southwest is its willingness to waste the human resources of minority groups.

As part of the teacher-training process, prospective teachers should be required to live and to work for a semester, perhaps in their junior year, in Mexican-American neighborhoods as teacher aides, tutors, social worker aides, and community organizer aides. They must be thoroughly exposed in a systematic and trained way to the social and economic environment from which their students come. And finally, they should receive a thorough training in the Spanish language, Mexican and Mexican-American history, culture, and values; the sociology of poverty; the teaching of English as a second language; and the special educational techniques required to educate non-English-speaking Mexican-American children.

The Acute Problems of the Southwest

Prejudice and discrimination pervade every aspect of Mexican-American life. Conditions are far worse in Texas than in other states, but no state is free of it. Indeed, the entire economic system of the Southwest is built upon economic exploitation of poorly paid Mexican-American workers in mining, in industry, and particularly in agriculture.

Thousands of Mexican-American school children in Texas, New Mexico, and California are taken out of the schools in April to migrate with their parents through the harvest fields of the West. They usually return to school in late October or early November. Many of them will have attended fifteen or twenty different schools before they drop out. Very few migrant children ever finish high school.

Many state departments of education such as the Texas Educational Agency have sponsored special educational programs for migrant children. They range from segregated migrant schools to segregated classes within regular school buildings. In all of them the school day is lengthened, and school meets on Saturdays and holidays to make up for lost time. Individual tutoring is often provided. In some of the schools, special innovative bilingual programs are found and in others the approach is more traditional. Almost all of these programs have had little success in retaining the migrant child in school.

After working with migrants for many years, the author is persuaded that two major innovations for the successful education of migrant children have considerable promise. One is the development of migrant teaching teams, equipped with paraprofessionals drawn from the ranks of migrant labor and with specially designed buses to move with the migrant workers through the migrant stream. The other technique is to compensate migrant families for the potential earning ability of their children, providing the children are kept in school.

It is essential to find solutions, for the problems are growing more acute. Mechanization of agriculture is accelerating. The migrants are well aware of the terminal nature of their occupation. More and more of them are concerned about the fate of their children. Large numbers of migrants are trying to settle out of the migrant stream wherever they can find permanent employment. Little clusters of former migrants are now appearing throughout the Midwest and the West.

The migrant stream will probably continue long enough to provide seasonable employment for the older migrants, but it may well collapse within ten years. It is highly essential that migrant children be given an education adequate enough to enable them to find employment outside the stream, or the

United States may be faced with thousands of stranded, unemployable migrants. The problem is worsened by the continual entrance into the stream of numerous Mexican immigrant families.

The social and economic plight of the Mexican-Americans can be seen nowhere more vividly than in northern New Mexico. This is one of the most beautiful mountainous regions in the United States, possessing the same natural resources found in Switzerland; it is also one of the poorest regions in the country. Conditions of poverty and malnutrition in the area resemble those of the poorer regions of Latin America than they do other parts of the rest of the United States.[20]

With their severely inadequate tax revenues and their inability to secure a more equitable distribution of state school funds, the school districts of this region lack the financial base to provide more than a semblance of an education. In northern New Mexico school districts, the dropout often approaches 80 per cent. Many of these school districts are unable to secure accreditation. Even the Santa Fe school district, located in the state capital, struggles continuously to secure minimal accreditation. The school districts located in the Anglo-American segments of the state usually have more money to spend on their athletic programs and gymnasiums than the Spanish-American school districts have available for their entire school operation. It is useless to discuss the possibilities of innovative programs for the Spanish-American school districts until they secure adequate funding.

Because of the distressed economic conditions of northern New Mexico, the poorly educated products of the northern school districts are forced to migrate to the metropolitan centers of New Mexico and other western states. Lacking the skills to compete effectively in the job market, they intensify the urban problems of the cities into which they migrate. Providing adequate funding for innovative educational programs to improve the educational quality of the urban bound immigrants from northern New Mexico would diminish the intensity of urban problems throughout the West.

The problems of the school districts are compounded by county political machines of which the schools are often a basic part. Teachers, principals, and bus drivers are given employment based not on their educational qualifications but on their voting patterns. Bus routes are extended or contracted according to the vote of small groups of villagers. Buildings are built by contractors who kick back to the political leaders. School supplies are purchased from favored merchants who contribute to the political campaign chest. Insurance on the physical plant is held by politicians who also control contracting firms and supply merchants. Academic programs are often supported or rejected according to the political status of those supporting programs.

Any attempt to improve these conditions meets with the organized resistance of local and state politicians who benefit from their continued existence. Many of these political leaders are opposed to any improvement in education, believing that a better educated electorate would vote them out of office. The refusal of the state government under both political parties to improve economic and educational opportunities in these counties is puzzling unless viewed in the light of the fact that a culturally isolated, Spanish-speaking, impoverished population is essential to the political good fortunes of many state politicians, who thus can afford to neglect the Spanish-speaking north and lavish their attention upon the Anglo-American south and east.

The question of integration versus segregation is a moot point in most of the Southwest. The majority of Mexican-American children attend segregated schools. There are few Anglo-American inhabitants in many regions of the Southwest such as northern New Mexico. In many urban centers into which Mexican-American immigrants are moving, neighborhood residential segregation creates segregated schools. Federal pressures and the civil rights movement are moving toward the elimination of neighborhood segregated schools through busing, pairing of schools, central assignment of school children, central educational parks, and other devices. Middle-class Mexican-American parents can be expected to favor and to encourage integration. However, the majority of poor Mexican-Americans have an intense loyalty to their local neighborhoods and would resent very much having strangers bused into their neighborhood schools or to have these schools closed in the name of integration. One can anticipate class conflicts and the rise of bitterness and hostility within Mexican-American communities over the issue of integration.

If integration comes, Mexican-American students must be assigned in large enough numbers to the various schools to warrant the special educational programs that they need. If this is not done, the excessively high dropout rate among Mexican-American students will increase to even higher levels. They could very well be sacrificed upon the altar of mechanical integration.

In summary, the present educational system from the university down to the first grade has failed to educate the Mexican-American. The social consequences of this failure are serious for society and for the Mexican-American. Society suffers from the loss of the contributions that Mexican-Americans might make to social welfare; from the movement of masses of poorly educated and poorly trained Mexican-Americans moving into the urban centers of the Southwest, the Rocky Mountains, and the Pacific Coast; and from the dangers of rising unrest and possibilities of violence.

Every Mexican-American neighborhood is filled with numbers of young Mexican-American males who are school dropouts and who are unemployed (indeed unemployable) and culturally marginal to both the Mexican-American and the Anglo-American societies. They are the raw material for social protest movements. The Mexican-Americans suffer from being entrapped in a social system that exploits them, denies them opportunities for social mobility and development of their capabilities, humiliates them, and rejects their language and culture. In the long run, any social system encounters danger from the existence of a large poverty-stricken population alienated from its values, unable to participate in its affluence, and lacking any loyalty or commitment to its continuance.

Notes

Chapter 1. The Meanings of Equality (pages 3-33)

1. Thomas Paine, *The Political Writings of Thomas Paine*, a new edition with additions (Boston: J. P. Mendum, 1856), Vol. 1, pp. 454-455.

2. Alexis de Tocqueville, *Democracy in America*, the Henry Reeve text as revised by Franicis Bowen (and) now further corrected and edited by Phillips Bradley (New York: Knopf, 1945), Vol. 2, pp. 96-97.

3. John Dewey, *The Public and Its Problems* (New York: Holt, 1927), pp. 150-151.

4. Carl J. Friedrich, "A Brief Discourse on the Origin of Political Equality," in J. Roland Pennock and John W. Chapman, eds., *Equality* (New York: Atherton Press, 1967), p. 220.

5. Horace Mann, *Education and Prosperity*, from his twelfth annual report as secretary of the Massachusetts State Board of Education, 1848, Old South Leaflets, Vol. 6, No. 144 (Boston: Directors of the Old South Work, 1903) p. 6.

6. *Plessy v. Ferguson*, 163 U.S. 538, 554, 559 (1896).

7. *Brown v. Board of Education of Topeka*, 347 U.S. 483, 493 (1954).

8. *Ibid.*, 495.

9. Anthony Downs, *Who Are the Urban Poor?* Rev. ed., CED Supplementary Paper No. 26, pp. 51, 55; U. S. Bureau of the Census, Current Population Reports: *Selected Characteristics of Persons and Families; March 1970*, Series P-20, No. 204, p. 12; *Median Family Income Up in 1970*, Series P-60, No. 78, p. 1; and *Employment and Earnings* (January 1971), p. 37 (Washington, D. C.: U. S. Government Printing Office.)

10. Thomas F. Pettigrew, "School Integration in Current Perspective," *The Urban Review*, Vol. 3, No. 3 (January 1969), p. 4.

11. *Statistical Abstract of the United States*, 91st ed., pp. 53, 685; U. S. Bureau of the Census, Current Population Reports: *Characteristics of American Youth*, Series P-23, No. 30, p. 9; *Median Family Income Up in 1970*, Series P-60, No. 78, p. 3; *Poverty Increases by 1.2 Million in 1970*, Series P-60, No. 77, p. 1; *Trends in Social and Economic Conditions in Metropolitan and Nonmetropolitan Areas*, Series P-23, No. 33, p. 38. (Washington, D. C.: U. S. Government Printing Office.)

12. U.S. Commission on Civil Rights, *Racial Isolation in the Public Schools* (Washington, D.C.: U.S. Government Printing Office, 1967), Vol. 1, p. 138.

13. Arthur Jensen, "How Much Can We Boost IQ and Scholastic Achievement?" *Harvard Educational Review*, Vol. 39, No. 1 (Winter 1969), p. 60.

14. James S. Coleman and others, *Equality of Educational Opportunity* (Washington, D.C.: U.S. Government Printing Office, 1966), p. 22.

15. Rockefeller Brothers Fund, *The Pursuit of Excellence; Education and the Future of America* (Garden City: Doubleday, 1958), pp. 28-29.

16. John H. Schaar, "Equality of Opportunity, and Beyond," in J. Roland Pennock and John W. Chapman, eds., *op. cit.* (note 4), pp. 229, 230.

17. Robert Rosenthal and Lenore Jacobson, *Pygmalion in the Classroom; Teacher Expectation and Pupils' Intellectual Development* (New York: Holt, Rinehart & Winston, 1968).

18. David Krech, "Psychoneurobiochemeducation," *Phi Delta Kappan*, Vol. 50, No. 7 (March 1969), pp. 370-374.

19. Erik H. Erikson, "The Concept of Identity in Race Relations: Notes and Queries," *Daedalus* (Winter 1966), p. 156.

Chapter 2. Poverty and Childhood (*pages 34-65*)

1. Susan S. Stodolsky and Gerald Lesser, "Learning Patterns in the Disadvantaged," *Harvard Educational Review*, Vol. 37, No. 4 (1967), pp. 546-593.

2. Benjamin S. Bloom, *Stability and Change in Human Characteristics* (New York: Wiley, 1964).

3. Jerome S. Bruner, "Origins of Problem Solving Strategies in Skill Acquisition," paper presented at the 19th International Congress of Psychology, London, July 1969; and Jerome S. Bruner and others, *Studies in the Growth of Manual Intelligence in Infancy*, Monographs of the Society for Research in Child Development (forthcoming).

4. Oscar Lewis, "The Culture of Poverty," *Scientific American*, Vol. 215, No. 4 (October 1966), pp. 19-25.

5. Robert D. Hess and Virginia C. Shipman, "Maternal Influences upon Early Learning: the Cognitive Environments of Urban Pre-School Children," in *Conference on Pre-School Education, Early Education; Current Theory, Research, and Action* (Chicago: Aldine, 1968).

6. James Moffett, *Teaching the Universe of Discourse* (Boston: Houghton Mifflin, 1968).

7. William Labov, *The Logic of Non-Standard English*, Georgetown Monograph series on Language and Linguistics, No. 22 (1969).

8. T. E. Strandberg and J. Griffith, *A Study of the Effects of Training in Visual Literacy on Verbal Language Behavior* (Eastern Illinois University, 1968).

9. Ilze Kalnins, "The Use of Sucking in Instrumental Learning," doctoral thesis (University of Toronto, 1970).

10. H. Papousek, "Experimental Studies of Appetitional Behavior in Human Newborns and Infants," in Harold W. Stevenson and others, eds., *Early Behavior; Comparative and Developmental Approaches* (New York: Wiley, 1967); and Lewis P. Lipsitt, "Learning in the Human Infant," in Harold W. Stevenson and others, eds., *op. cit.*

11. E. von Holst and H. Mittelstaedt, "Das Reafferenzprinzip," *Naturwissenschaften*, 37 (1950), pp. 464-476.

12. R. Held and A. V. Hein, "Adaptation of Disarranged Hand-Eye Coordination Contingent upon Re-Afferent Stimulation," *Perceptual and Motor Skills*, 8 (1958), pp. 87-90.

13. Jean Piaget, *The Construction of Reality in the Child* (New York: Basic Books, 1954).

14. L. S. Vygotsky, *Thought and Language* (Cambridge: M.I.T. Press, 1962).

15. Patricia M. Greenfield, "Goal as Environmental Variable in the Development of Intelligence," paper presented at the Conference on Contributions to Intelligence, University of Illinois, Urbana, November 15, 1969.

16. Robert D. Hess and others, *The Cognitive Environments of Urban Preschool Children* (University of Chicago, 1969).

17. Maxine Schoggen, *An Ecological Study of Three-Year-Olds at Home* (George Peabody College for Teachers, 1969); and Rupert A. Klaus and Susan W. Gray, *The Early Training Project for Disadvantaged Children; a Report After Five Years* (Chicago: Published by the University of Chicago Press for the Society for Research in Child Development, 1968).

18. Robert D. Hess and Virginia C. Shipman, "Early Experience and Socialization of Cognitive Modes in Children," *Child Development*, 36 (1965), pp. 869-886; Helen L. Bee and others, "Social Class Differences in Maternal Teaching Strategies and Speech Patterns," *Developmental Psychology*, Vol. 1 No. 6 (1969), pp. 726-734.

19. Jerome Kagan and Howard A. Moss, *Birth to Maturity, a Study in Psychological Development* (New York: Wiley, 1962).

20. H. B. Robinson and N. M. Robinson, "The Problem of Timing in Preschool Education," in Conference on Pre-School Education, *op. cit.* (note 5).

21. Nancy B. Graves, *City, Country, and Child Rearing in Three Cultures* (University of Colorado, 1969).

22. Warren Haggstrom, "The Power of the Poor," in Frank Riessman and others, eds., *Mental Health of the Poor; New Treatment Approaches for Low Income People* (New York: Free Press of Glencoe, 1964).

23. Robert D. Hess and Virginia C. Shipman, *op. cit.* (note 18); and Basil Bernstein, "Social Class and Linguistic Development: a Theory of Social

Learning," in A. H. Halsey and others, eds., *Education, Economy, and Society* (New York: Free Press of Glencoe, 1961).

24. Helen L. Bee and others, *op. cit.* (note 18).

25. Robert D. Hess and Virginia C. Shipman, *op. cit.* (note 18).

26. E. Zigler and E. Butterfield, "Motivational Aspects of Changes in IQ Test Performance of Culturally Deprived Nursery School Children," *Child Development*, 39 (1968), pp. 1-14.

27. G. J. Turner and R. E. Pickvance, *Social Class Differences in the Expression of Uncertainty in Five-Year-Old Children* (University of London, 1970).

28. Rupert A. Klaus and Susan W. Gray, *op. cit.* (note 17); W. P. Robinson and C. D. Creed, "Perceptual and Verbal Discriminations of 'Elaborated' and 'Restricted' Code Users," *Language and Speech*, 2 (1968), pp. 182-193.

29. Marion Blank and Frances Solomon, "How Shall the Disadvantaged Child Be Taught?" *Child Development*, 40 (1969), pp. 47-61.

30. Earl S. Schaefer, "Need for Early and Continuing Education," in *Education of the Infant and Young Child*, ed. by Victor H. Denenberg (New York: Academic Press, 1970).

31. Courtney B. Cazden, "Language Education: Learning That, Learning How, Learning To," paper presented at the Boston Colloquium for the Philosophy of Education, Boston University, Boston, April 13, 1970.

32. R. Brown and others, "The Child's Grammar from I to III," in *Minnesota Symposium on Child Psychology*, ed. by John P. Hill (Minneapolis: University of Minnesota Press, 1969); Vivian M. Horner, "The Verbal World of the Lower-Class Three-Year-Old: a Pilot Study in Linguistic Ecology," doctoral thesis (University of Rochester, 1968); and Dan I. Slobin, "Questions of Language Development in Cross-Cultural Perspective," paper presented at Symposium on Language Learning in Cross-Cultural Perspective, Michigan State University, East Lansing, September 1968.

33. James S. Coleman and others, *Equality of Educational Opportunity* (Washington, D.C.: U.S. Government Printing Office, 1966).

34. Joan Tough, *An Interim Report of a Longitudinal Study* (University of Leeds, 1970).

35. Rupert A. Klaus and Susan W. Gray, *op. cit.* (note 17).

36. Basil Bernstein, "Social Class, Language, and Socialization" (1970).

37. Jerome S. Bruner and others, *A Study of Thinking* (New York: Wiley, 1956).

38. Courtney B. Cazden, "Situation: a Neglected Source of Social Class Differences in Language Use," *Journal of Social Issues*, 26 (Spring 1970), pp. 35-60; and William Labov, *op. cit.* (note 7).

39. D. Hymes, "On Communication Competence," in R. Huxley and E. Ingram, eds., *The Mechanism of Language Development* (London: Ciba Foundation, forthcoming).

40. E. R. Heider and others, *Social Class Differences in the Effectiveness and Style of Children's Coding Ability* (New York: Cornell University, 1968).

41. Francis Palmer, unpublished research cited in J. S. Kagan, "Inadequate Evidence and Illogical Conclusions," *Harvard Educational Review*, Vol. 39, No. 2 (1969), pp. 274-277.

42. William Labov, *op. cit.* (note 7).
43. Grace de Laguna, *Speech, Its Function and Development* (New Haven: Yale University Press, 1927).
44. Jerrold J. Katz and Jerry A. Fodor, "The Structure of a Semantic Theory," in Jerry A. Fodor and Jerrold J. Katz, eds., *The Structure of Language: Readings in the Philosophy of Language* (Englewood Cliffs: Prentice-Hall, 1964).
45. Patricia M. Greenfield, "Oral or Written Language: the Consequence for Cognitive Development in Africa and the United States," paper presented at Symposium on Cross-Cultural Cognitive Studies, American Educational Research Association, Chicago, February 9, 1968.
46. Basil Bernstein, *op. cit.* (note 36).
47. Joan Tough, *op. cit.* (note 34).
48. P. R. Hawkins, *Social Class, the Nominal Group, and Reference* (University of London, 1968).
49. Basil Bernstein, *op. cit.* (note 36).
50. Helen L. Bee and others, *op. cit.* (note 18); L. Kohlberg, "Early Education: a Cognitive-Developmental View," *Child Development*, 39 (1968), pp. 1013-1062; and P. R. Hawkins, *op. cit.* (note 48).
51. D. Hamburg, "Evolution of Emotional Responses: Evidence from Recent Research on Nonhuman Primates," in American Academy of Psychoanalysis, *Animal and Human* (New York: Grune & Stratton, 1968).
52. Meyer Fortes, *Social and Psychological Aspects of Education in Taleland* (London: Published by the Oxford University Press for the International Institute of African Languages and Culture, 1938); and Elizabeth Marshall Thomas, "The Bushmen of Kalahari," *National Geographic Magazine*, Vol. 123, No. 6 (June 1963), pp. 866-888.
53. R. Brown and others, *op. cit.* (note 32).
54. Sarah Smilansky, "The Effect of Certain Learning Conditions on the Progress of Disadvantaged Children of Kindergarten Age," *Journal of School Psychology*, Vol. 4, No. 3 (1968), pp. 68-81.
55. Stephen S. Baratz and Joan C. Baratz, "Early Childhood Intervention: the Social Science Base of Institutional Racism," *Harvard Educational Review*, Vol. 40, No. 1 (1970), pp. 29-50.
56. James S. Coleman and others, *op. cit.* (note 33).
57. Jean Piaget, *The Origins of Intelligence in Children* (New York: International Universities Press, 1952).
58. Hans Aebli, paper presented at the Center for Cognitive Studies, Harvard University, Cambridge, June 5, 1970.
59. J. M. Sugarman, "The Future of Early Childhood Programs: an American Perspective" (1970).
60. Victor G. Cicirelli and others, *The Impact of Head Start: an Evaluation of the Effects of Head Start on Children's Cognitive and Affective Development* (Westinghouse Learning Corporation and Ohio University, 1969); Robert Rosenthal and Lenore Jacobson, *Pygmalion in the Classroom; Teacher*

Expectation and Pupils' Intellectual Development (New York: Holt, Rinehart & Winston, 1968); and Nancy B. Graves, *op. cit.* (note 21).

61.   Warren Haggstrom, *op. cit.* (note 22).

Chapter 3. The Crucible of the Urban Classroom (*pages 66-103*)

1.   Edgar Z. Friedenberg, "The Generation Gap," *The Annals of The American Academy of Political and Social Science*, Vol. 382 (March 1969), pp. 33-34.

2.   *Ibid.*, p. 34.

3.   *Ibid.*, p. 38.

4.   Rudolf Dreikurs and Loren Grey, *Logical Consequences; a New Approach to Discipline* (New York: Hawthorn Books, 1968), p. 11.

5.   Richard A. Cloward and Lloyd E. Ohlin, *Delinquency and Opportunity; a Theory of Delinquent Gangs* (Glencoe: Free Press, 1960), pp. 161-186.

6.   Charles V. Willie, "Anti-Social Behavior Among Disadvantaged Youth," *Journal of Negro Education*, Vol. 33, No. 2 (Spring 1964), pp. 176-181.

7.   *Ibid.*

8.   Raymond W. Mack, "The Changing Ethnic Fabric of the Metropolis," in Bobby J. Chandler and others, eds., *Education in Urban Society* (New York: Dodd, Mead, 1962), pp. 54-69.

9.   Staten W. Webster, *Discipline in the Classroom; Basic Principles and Problems* (San Francisco: Chandler, 1968), pp. 16-21.

10.   Thomas S. Langner, "SES and Personality Characteristics," in Thomas S. Langner and Stanley T. Michael, *Life Stress and Mental Health* (New York: Free Press of Glencoe, 1963), pp. 436-475.

11.   David Ausubel and Pearl Ausubel, "Ego Development Among Segregated Negro Children," in Work Conference on Curriculum and Teaching in Depressed Urban Areas, Columbia University, *Education in Depressed Areas* (New York: Teachers College, 1963), pp. 113-141.

12.   Urie Bronfenbrenner, "Socialization and Social Class Through Time and Space," in Society for the Psychological Study of Social Issues, *Readings in Social Psychology*, 3rd ed. (New York: Holt, Rinehart & Winston, 1958), pp. 400-425.

13.   *Ibid.*, p. 420.

14.   *Ibid.*, pp. 423-425.

15.   Norma Radin and Constance Kamii, "The Child-Rearing Attitudes of Disadvantaged Negro Mothers and Some Educational Implications," *Journal of Negro Education*, Vol. 34, No. 2 (Spring 1965), pp. 138-146.

16.   Albert K. Cohen, *Delinquent Boys; the Culture of the Gang* (Glencoe: Free Press, 1955), pp. 88-93.

17.   Allison Davis and Robert J. Havighurst, "Social Class and Color Differences in Child-Rearing," *American Sociological Review*, Vol. 11, No. 6 (December 1946), pp. 698-710.

18. Thomas S. Langner, *op. cit.* (note 10).

19. *Ibid.*

20. David Ausubel and Pearl Ausubel, *op. cit.* (note 11); and Urie Bronfen-brenner, *op. cit.* (note 12).

21. Thomas S. Langner, *op. cit.* (note 10).

22. H. Wortis, "Child Rearing Practices in a Low Socio-Economic Group," *Pediatrics*, Vol. 32, No. 2 (August 1963), pp. 298-307.

23. Frances R. Link, "Pressures on Youth: Suburbia," *Theory Into Practice*, Vol. 7, No. 1 (February 1968), pp. 23-25.

24. *Ibid.*, p. 24.

25. David Ausubel and Pearl Ausubel, *op. cit.* (note 11).

26. Elizabeth Douvan, "Social Status and Success Strivings," *Journal of Abnormal and Social Psychology*, Vol. 52, No. 2 (March 1956), pp. 219-224.

27. Walter B. Miller, "Lower Class Culture as a Generating Milieu of Gang Delinquency," *Journal of Social Issues*, Vol. 14, No. 3 (1958), pp. 5-19.

28. Kurt Lewin, *Resolving Social Conflicts* (New York: Harper & Row, 1948), pp. 56-68.

29. Mario D. Fantini and Gerald Weinstein, *The Disadvantaged: Challenge to Education* (New York Harper & Row, 1968), pp. 304-335.

30. Erich Fromm, *The Art of Loving* (New York: Harper & Row, 1956).

31. Carl Rogers, "The Facilitation of Significant Learning," in Laurence Siegel, *Instruction: Some Contemporary Viewpoints* (San Francisco: Chandler, 1967), pp. 37-54.

32. Nathaniel Hickerson, *Education for Alienation* (Englewood Cliffs: Prentice-Hall, 1966).

33. Mario D. Fantini and Gerald Weinstein, *Toward a Contract Curriculum* (New York: Anti-Defamation League of B'nai B'rith, 1967).

34. Mario D. Fantini and Gerald Weinstein, *op. cit.* (note 29), pp. 131-139.

Chapter 4. Increasing Educational Opportunity (pages 104-121)

1. James S. Coleman and others, *Equality of Educational Opportunity* (Washington, D.C.: U.S. Government Printing Office, 1966).

2. Frederick Mosteller and Daniel P. Moynihan, eds., *On Equality of Educational Opportunity* (New York: Random House, forthcoming).

3. U.S. Commission on Civil Rights, *Racial Isolation in the Public Schools* (Washington, D.C.: U.S. Government Printing Office, 1967).

4. James M. McPartland, *The Segregated Student in Desegregated Schools: Sources of Influence on Negro Secondary Students* (Baltimore: Johns Hopkins University, 1968).

5. Samuel Bowles and Henry M. Levin, "The Determinants of Scholastic Achievement—an Appraisal of Some Recent Evidence," *Journal of Human*

Resources, Vol. 3, No. 1 (Winter 1968), pp. 3-24; James S. Coleman, "Equality of Educational Opportunity: Reply to Bowles and Levin," *Journal of Human Resources*, Vol 3, No. 2 (Spring 1968), pp. 237-246; Glen G. Cain and Harold W. Watts, "Problems in Making Policy Inferences from the Coleman Report," *American Sociological Review*, Vol. 35, No. 2 (April 1970), pp. 228-242; James S. Coleman, "Reply to Cain and Watts," *American Sociological Review*, Vol. 35, No. 2 (April 1970), pp. 242-249; and Eric A. Hanushek and John F. Kain, "On the Value of Equality of Educational Opportunity as a Guide to Public Policy," in Frederick Mosteller and Daniel P. Moynihan, eds., *op. cit.* (note 2).

6. George W. Mayeske and others, *A Study of Our Nation's Schools* (Washington, D.C.: U.S. Office of Education, 1969).

7. Robert P. O'Reilly and others, *Racial and Social Class Isolation in the Schools* (University of the State of New York, 1969).

8. David J. Fox, *Expansion of the More Effective Schools Program* (New York: Center for Urban Education, 1967).

9. Victor G. Cicirelli and others, *The Impact of Head Start: an Evaluation of the Effects of Head Start on Children's Cognitive and Affective Development* (Westinghouse Learning Corporation and Ohio University, 1969).

10. Benjamin S. Bloom, *Stability and Change in Human Characteristics* (New York: Wiley, 1964).

Chapter 5. Relevance and Self-Image (pages 122-141)

1. Martin Deutsch, *Minority Group and Class Status as Related to Social and Personality Factors in Scholastic Achievement* (Ithaca: Society for Applied Anthropology, 1960).

2. Irwin Katz, "Review of Evidence Relating to Effects of Desegregation on the Intellectual Performance of Negroes," *American Psychologist*, Vol. 19, No. 6 (June 1964), pp. 381-399.

3. Martin Deutsch, *op. cit.* (note 1).

4. Monroe W. Karmin, "Ethnic Power: Nationality Groups Aim To Vie with Negroes for Government Aid," *The Wall Street Journal* (April 24, 1969), pp. 1, 16.

5. Andrew F. Brimmer, " 'Black Studies;' a Top Negro's View," *U.S. News & World Report*, Vol. 67, No. 10 (September 8, 1969), p. 12.

6. S. Samuel Shermis, "Six Myths Which Delude History Teachers" (1968).

7. Richard A. Schmuck and Philip J. Runkel, *Organizational Training for a School Faculty* (Eugene: University of Oregon, Center for the Advanced Study of Educational Administration, 1970).

8. Ronald C. Bigelow, *The Effect of Organizational Development on Classroom Climate* (Eugene: University of Oregon, Center for the Advanced Study of Educational Administration, 1969).

Chapter 6. Problems of the Mexican-Americans (pages 142-180)

1. Although somewhat dated, the best study on the Mexican-American people
    is still Carey McWilliams, *North from Mexico; the Spanish-Speaking People of
    the United States* (Philadelphia: Lippincott, 1948). See also John H. Burma,
    Spanish-Speaking Groups in the United States (Durham: Duke University
    Press, 1954); Harley L. Browning and S. Dale McLemore, *A Statistical
    Profile of the Spanish-Surname Population of Texas* (Austin: University of
    Texas, Bureau of Business Research, 1964); Margaret Clark, *Health in the
    Mexican American Culture; a Community Study* (Berkeley: University of
    California Press, 1959); Clark S. Knowlton, "The Spanish Americans in
    New Mexico," *Sociology and Social Research*, 45 (July 1961), pp. 448-454;
    William Madsen, *Mexican-Americans of South Texas* (New York: Holt,
    Rinehart & Winston, 1964); Arthur J. Rubel, *Across the Tracks; Mexican-
    Americans in a Texas City* (Austin: University of Texas Press, 1966); Lyle
    Saunders, *Cultural Difference and Medical Care; the Case of the Spanish-
    Speaking People of the Southwest* (New York: Russell Sage Foundation,
    1954); Julian Samora, ed., *La Raza; Forgotten Americans* (South Bend:
    University of Notre Dame Press, 1966); and George I. Sanchez, *Forgotten
    People; a Study of New Mexicans* (Albuquerque: University of New Mexico
    Press, 1940).

2. Ralph Yarborough, "Two Proposals for a Better Way of Life for Mexican-
    Americans of the Southwest," in U.S. Congress, *Congressional Record*
    (Washington, D.C.: U.S. Government Printing Office, 1967), Vol. 113,
    Part 1, p. 599.

3. Faye L. Bumpass, "Supplemental Statement: Mexican American Educational
    Problems in the Southwest," in U.S. Congress. Senate. Committee on Labor
    and Public Welfare, *Bilingual Education*, hearings before the Special Sub-
    committee on Bilingual Education (Washington, D.C.: U.S. Government
    Printing Office, 1967), Part 1, pp. 67-71.

4. *Ibid.*

5. *Ibid.*

6. Data supplied by a staff member of the Salt Lake City school district.

7. For discussions of programs that have failed, see Interagency Council for
    Area Development Planning and New Mexico State Planning Office, *Embudo:
    a Pilot Planning Project for the Embudo Watershed of New Mexico* (n.d.);
    and Clark S. Knowlton, "Area Development and Planning in New Mexico:
    Implications for Dependency and for Economic and Social Growth," in U.S.
    Congress. House. Committee on Agriculture, *Effect of Federal Programs on
    Rural America*, hearings before the Subcommittee on Rural Development
    (Washington, D.C.: U.S. Government Printing Office, 1967).

8. Clark S. Knowlton, "Problems and Difficulties in Planning and Development
    in Areas with Large Minority Groups," paper prepared for the Southern
    Sociological Society, April 17, 1964.

9. For analyses of the educational needs and problems of the Mexican-
    Americans, see Herschel T. Manuel, *Spanish-Speaking Children of the South-
    west: Their Education and the Public Welfare* (Austin: University of Texas

Press, 1965); Lloyd S. Tireman and Mary Watson, *A Community School in a Spanish-Speaking Village* (Albuquerque: University of New Mexico Press, 1948); Horacio Ulibarri, *The Effect of Cultural Difference in the Education of Spanish-Americans* (Albuquerque: University of New Mexico, College of Education, 1958); Miles V. Zintz, *Education Across Cultures* (Dubuque: W. C. Brown Book Co., 1963); Leo Grebler, *The Schooling Gap: Signs of Progress*, Mexican-American Study Project, Advance Report 7 (Los Angeles: University of California, 1967); Paul Seldon, "Mexican-Americans in Urban Schools," in *The Laboratory in Urban Culture* (Los Angeles: Occidental College, 1959); and Celia S. Heller, *Mexican American Youth; Forgotten Youth at the Crossroads* (New York: Random House, 1966).

10. For good histories of the Southwest, see Lynn I. Perrigo, *Texas and Our Spanish Southwest* (Dallas: Banks Upshaw and Co., 1960); William Eugene Hollon, *The Southwest: Old and New* (New York: Knopf, 1961); and Howard R. Lamar, *The Far Southwest, 1846-1912; a Territorial History* (New Haven: Yale University Press, 1966).

11. John H. Culley, *Cattle, Horses and Men of the Western Range* (Los Angeles: Ward Ritchie Press, 1940).

12. Although no study has been made of segregation affecting the Mexican-Americans, the following have pertinent information: Carey McWilliams, *op. cit.* (note 1); William Madsen, *op. cit.* (note 1); and Arthur J. Rubel, *op. cit.* (note 1).

13. Clark S. Knowlton, "One Approach to the Economic and Social Problems of Northern New Mexico," *New Mexico Business*, 17 (September 1964), pp. 3, 15-22; Carey McWilliams, *op. cit.* (note 1); Harley L. Browning and S. Dale McLemore, *op. cit.* (note 1); and George I. Sanchez, *op. cit.* (note 1).

14. For material on the bilingual approach to the education of the Mexican-American child, see A. Bruce Gardner and others, "The Challenge of Bilingualism," in Northeast Conference on the Teaching of Foreign Languages, *Foreign Language Teaching: Challenges to the Profession* (1965); Wallace Lambert and Elizabeth Peal, "The Relation of Bilingualism to Intelligence," *Psychological Monographs: General and Applied*, 76 (1962); and James McNab Christian and Chester C. Christian, Jr., "Spanish Language and Culture in the Southwest," in Joshua A. Fishman, *Language Loyalty in the United States* (The Hague: Mouton and Co , 1966), pp. 280-317. For data on the educational needs and problems of the Mexican-Americans and on various aspects of bilingual education, see U.S. Congress. Senate. Committee on Labor and Public Welfare, *op. cit.* (note 3); and U.S. Congress. House. Committee on Education and Labor, *Bilingual Education Programs*, hearings before the General Subcommittee on Education (Washington, D.C.: U.S. Government Printing Office, 1967).

15. For material on ongoing bilingual programs affecting Spanish-speaking Children, see the reports in U.S. Congress. Senate. Committee on Labor and Public Welfare, *op. cit.* (note 3); and U.S. Congress. House. Committee on Education and Labor, *op. cit.* (note 14).

16. Holding S. Carlson and Norma Henderson, "Intelligence of American Children of Mexican Parentage," *Journal of Abnormal and Social Psychology*

45 (April 1952), pp. 544-551; J. M. Cook and Grace Arthur, "Intelligence Rating of 97 Mexican-Americans in St. Paul," *Journal of Exceptional Children*, 18 (October 1951), pp. 14-15; Natalie T. Darcy, "A Review of the Literature on the Effects of Bi-Lingualism upon the Measurement of Intelligence," *Journal of Genetic Psychology*, 82 (January 1953), pp. 21-27; Arthur Jensen, "Learning Abilities in Mexican-American Children," *California Journal of Educational Research*, 12 (September 1961), pp. 147-159; M. J. Keston and C. A. Jimine, "A Study of the Performance on English and Spanish Edition of the Stanford-Binet Intelligence Test by Spanish-American Children," *Journal of Genetic Psychology*, 85 (December 1954), pp. 263-269; and Bernard Spilka and Lois Gill, "Some Non-Intellectual Correlates of Academic Achievement Among Spanish-American Students," *School Counselor*, 12 (May 1965), pp. 218-221.

17. Stanley Lieberson, "Bilingualism in Montreal: a Demographic Analysis," *American Journal of Sociology*, 71 (July 1965), pp. 10-25.

18. Many reports on school districts in diverse sections of the country about special programs that have been developed to meet the special needs of bilingual student populations can be found in U.S. Congress. Senate. Committee on Labor and Public Welfare, *op. cit.* (note 3); and U.S. Congress. House. Committee on Education and Labor, *op. cit.* (note 14).

19. A. Bruce Gardner, "Our Bilinguals: Linguistic and Pedagogical Barriers," in Southwest Council of Foreign Language Teachers, *Reports, Our Bilinguals: Social and Psychological Barriers, Linguistic and Pedagogical Barriers* (1965).

20. For an excellent analysis of the problems and characteristics of a northern New Mexico school district, see National Education Association. National Commission on Professional Rights and Responsibilities, *Roi Arriba County, New Mexico, When Public Education Provides Patronage for a Political System* (Washington, D.C.: 1964).

Contributors

RONALD C. BIGELOW is a social psychologist who is now with the Peace Corps as a training and education specialist for the Latin American region. He has participated in all aspects of public education as a classroom teacher, department chairman, vice-principal, and researcher. He has also been involved in teacher training and curriculum development. Bigelow completed his undergraduate studies at the University of Oregon in 1961 and received a master's degree at Oregon State University in 1966, returning to the University of Oregon to earn a doctorate in education, research, and social psychology in 1969. Before joining the Peace Corps in 1971, he served on the faculty of the University of Utah as an assistant professor.

JEROME S. BRUNER, director of the Center of Cognitive Studies at Harvard University, which he helped found in 1960, is one of the world's outstanding authorities on childhood development. He has served as an advisor to Presidential committees, the State Department, the Department of Defense, the United Nations, the National Science Foundation, and the National Institutes of Health. Bruner has been president of the American Psychological Association, and he is a founding fellow of the National Academy of Education, a fellow of the American Academy of Arts and Sciences, and a director of the John F. Kennedy Center for Research on Human Development. In the fall of 1972, after twenty-seven years on the Harvard faculty, he will become Watts Professor of Psychology at Oxford University. Among his writings are *The Process of Education*, *A Study of Thinking* (with Goodnow and Austin), *On Knowing: Essays for the Left Hand*, *Studies in Cognitive Growth* (with Olver, Greenfield, et al), *Toward a Theory of Instruction*, and *Processes of Cognitive Growth: Infancy*.

JAMES S. COLEMAN had the major responsibility for the design, administration, and analysis of the massive study of the availability of equal educational opportunities in the United States undertaken in 1965 by the National Center for Educational Statistics of the Office of Education. The resultant report, *Equality of Educational Opportunity*, is better known by his name. Coleman completed his undergraduate studies at Purdue University, received his doctorate in sociology from Columbia University in 1955, and became a fellow at the Center for Advanced Studies in the Behaviorial Sciences. He was on the faculty of the University of Chicago from 1956 to 1959 and is now a professor at Johns Hopkins University. He is the author of more than 100 books, monographs, and papers in a wide area of studies, including *Union Democracy* (with Seymour M. Lipset and Martin A. Trow), *Community Conflict, Social Climates in High Schools, Models of Change and Response Uncertainty, Adolescents and the Schools*, and *Medical Innovation* (with Elihu Katz and Herbert Menzel).

JAMES L. JARRETT is professor of philosophy of education and associate dean of the School of Education at the University of California at Berkeley. He graduated from the University of Utah and was a member of the faculty there from 1943 to 1955, meanwhile earning his doctorate in philosophy at the University of Michigan in 1948. After serving as regional director and then president of the Great Books Foundation, Jarrett was president of Western Washington State College from 1959 until he joined the Berkeley faculty in 1964. He has been chairman of the Research Advisory Council of the Office of Education, director of the Hazen Foundation Study of Undergraduate Teaching, and a member of the California State Curriculum Commission. His writings include *Quest for Beauty* and *The Educational Theories of the Sophists*, as well as numerous papers in scholarly journals and publications, and he has collaborated as an author and editor of books on philosophy and logic with Sterling M. McMurrin and Robert T. Harris.

CLARK S. KNOWLTON, professor of sociology at the University of Utah and director of the university's Center for the Study of Social Problems, is a leading authority on the social, economic, and cultural problems of the Mexican-Americans. He studied at Brigham Young University; the Escola Livre de Sociologia y Ciencias Socias in Sao Paulo, Brazil; and Vanderbilt University, where he received his doctoral degree in 1955. Knowlton has directed a number of studies and projects in the Southwest funded through government and university grants, among them a Department of Health, Education, and Welfare program to reduce juvenile delinquency in El Paso. He has been on the faculties of New Mexico Highlands University and Texas Western College, and he has also served as president of the Rocky Mountain Social Science Association. He has written and edited numerous papers, reports, and surveys concerning Mexican-American, American Indian, and Southwestern regional problems.

LARRY L. LESLIE is associate professor and chairman of higher education at Pennsylvania State University and also research associate at the university's Center for the Study of Higher Education. Prior to 1970 he taught in secondary schools in California and was assistant professor of education and director of student teaching at the University of Utah. A graduate of the University of Minnesota, Leslie received his doctorate in higher education from the University of California at Berkeley in 1968. His teaching, writing, and research have spanned the areas of administration of urban schools, teaching the disadvantaged, racial attitudes in the schools, education for the professions, and the accreditation process in universities. He has served as consultant and advisor to the Office of Economic Opportunity, the American Association for Teacher Education, and the Wyoming and Utah state boards of education.

STERLING M. MCMURRIN is E.E. Ericksen Distinguished Professor of the University of Utah and dean of the Graduate School. He has served on the faculty of the University of Southern California and has been visiting scholar at Columbia University and Union Theological Seminary and Ford fellow in philosophy at Princeton University. His wide government experience has included service as United States Commissioner of Education in 1961-62 and chairman of the Federal Commission on Instructional Technology. He is a trustee of the Carnegie Foundation and has been vice president of the American Philosophical Association. McMurrin has also served as a member of the CED Research Advisory Board and as project director of the recent CED studies on innovation in education and education for the urban disadvantaged. He is project director of the new subcommittee on the management and financing of colleges. His writings include *A History of Philosophy* (with B.A.G. Fuller) and *Contemporary Philosophy* (with James L. Jarrett).

STATEN W. WEBSTER, professor of education at the University of California at Berkeley, has had wide experience as a teacher of teachers and as a director of research studies concerned with minority and disadvantaged students. After completing his undergraduate work at Berkeley, he taught social studies in high schools for several years and then returned to the university as a supervisor of teacher education, earning his doctorate in education in 1960. Webster has conducted research projects for the California Commission on Public School Administration and the National Institute of Mental Health, and he has been advisor and consultant to various school systems and governmental bodies, including the U.S. Commission on Civil Rights. He has directed and produced several educational television series on human relations in the schools. Webster is the author of *Discipline in the Classroom* and the editor of *The Disadvantaged Learner: Knowing, Understanding, Educating.*

Index

Abilities
  acquired vs. inherited, 7
  relative value of, 11
Academic achievement
  causes of variations in, 107-113
  and compensatory programs,
    114-116
  and environment, 117-121
  role of self image in, 123
Acculturation, as educational goal,
    132, 165-166, 172
Achievement motivation, class
    differences in, 42, 43, 45-46, 54,
    85-87
Achievement tests, 97, 114, 116
  vs. vocabulary tests, 47
Adolescence
  developmental tasks in, 77-79
  extended, 70
  isolated status of, 73
Adult models, 79
  of class patterns, 54-56
  in low-income families, 80
Adults, child's independence of, 75,
    76, 77; *see also* Parents
Aebli, H., 57
Aggression, and class norms, 83, 89
Alienation
  as cause of antisocial behavior, 72
  in minority groups, 21, 72, 152, 153
  of students, 96, 97
American Indians, 107, 125
  and Mexican-Americans, 150
  in U.S. history, 132
Anti-semitism, 127
Antisocial behavior
  deprivation as cause of, 71-72
  maturation problems as cause of,
    76-77
Aristotle, 4, 5, 10, 14

Art of Loving, The (Fromm), 94
Austin, George A., 48
Ausubel, David and Pearl, 79-80, 86

Baratz, J. C. and S. S., 56
Beckwourth, James P., 129
Bee, Helen L., 42, 45, 54
Bellugi, U., 47, 55
Berlin, Isaiah, 6
Bernstein, Basil, 44, 46, 48, 51-52
Bilingualism, 162-163, 171
Black militancy, 21, 24, 72, 124
Black separatism, 124
Black studies programs, 124-126, 130
Blacks
  alienation of, 21, 72
  educability of, 26
  educational achievement of, 107,
    108, 118
  educational opportunities for, 24,
    26
  parent-child relationships of, 81-82
  post-bellum education of, 15-16
  self-acceptance of, 10
  socioeconomic conditions of,
    19-20, 72
  subcultural norms of, 87-90
Blank, Marion, 47
Bloom, Benjamin S., 35, 116-117
Bowles, Samuel, 112
Brimmer, Andrew F., 126
Bronfenbrenner, Urie, 80
Brown, R., 47, 49, 55
Brown v. Board of Education
    (1954), 16-18, 20
Butterfield, E., 46

Cain, Glen G., 112
Cazden, C. B., 47, 49, 55
Chavez, Cesar, 153
Chesterton, G. K., 6

197